# Python Web Development

## Django, Flask, and FastAPI for Building Robust Web Applications

## COPYRIGHT

© [2024] by All rights reserved.

No part of this publication may be reproduced, distributed, or transmitted in any form or by any means, including photocopying, recording, or other electronic or mechanical methods, without the prior written permission of the publisher, except in the case of brief quotations embodied in critical reviews and certain other noncommercial uses permitted by copyright law.

# Contents

**Chapter 1: Introduction to Python Web Development** ...... 4

    Understanding Web Development ........................... 4

    The Role of Python in Web Development ............... 5

    Exploring Popular Python Frameworks ................. 6

        Django: The High-Level Framework ................... 6

        Flask: The Lightweight Framework ..................... 7

        FastAPI: The Modern Framework ....................... 7

    The Importance of Frameworks ............................. 8

    Conclusion of Chapter 1 .......................................... 9

**Chapter 2: Setting Up Your Development Environment** ...... 11

    Installing Python ..................................................... 11

    Creating and Managing Virtual Environments ..... 12

    Managing Packages with pip ................................. 13

    Choosing an Integrated Development Environment (IDE) .................................................... 14

    Version Control with Git .......................................... 15

    Setting Up a Local Web Server ............................. 17

    Conclusion of Chapter 2 ........................................ 17

**Chapter 3: Introduction to Django** ............................ 19

    What is Django? ..................................................... 19

    Key Features of Django ......................................... 20

- 1. ORM (Object-Relational Mapping) .............. 20
- 2. Admin Interface .............................. 20
- 3. Authentication and Authorization ............. 21
- 4. URL Routing .................................. 22
- 5. Middleware Support ........................... 22
- 6. Security Features ............................ 23
- 7. Scalability and Performance .................. 23

Django's Architecture: The MVT Pattern ............ 24

- Model ........................................... 24
- View ............................................ 24
- Template ........................................ 25

The Philosophy of Django .......................... 25

Django's Ecosystem and Community .................. 26

Conclusion of Chapter 3 ........................... 27

Chapter 4: Setting Up a Django Project ............ 29

Creating a New Django Project ..................... 29

Understanding the Project Structure ............... 30

- 1. manage.py .................................... 31
- 2. settings.py .................................. 31
- 3. urls.py ...................................... 32
- 4. asgi.py and wsgi.py .......................... 32
- 5. __init__.py .................................. 33

Configuring Settings .............................. 33

- 1. Database Configuration ................................. 33
- 2. Allowed Hosts ............................................. 34
- 3. Static and Media Files ................................. 35
- 4. Installed Apps ............................................. 35

**Creating a Django App** ................................... 36
- 1. models.py .................................................... 37
- 2. views.py ...................................................... 38
- 3. admin.py ..................................................... 39

**Running the Development Server** .................. 39

**Conclusion of Chapter 4** ................................. 40

**Chapter 5: Django Models and the ORM** ....... 42

**Understanding Django Models** ...................... 42
- Creating a Model ............................................. 42
- Field Types ...................................................... 44
- Defining Relationships .................................... 44

**Database Migrations** ...................................... 46
- Creating Migrations ......................................... 47
- Applying Migrations ........................................ 47

**Querying the Database with the ORM** .......... 48
- Retrieving Objects ........................................... 48
- Creating and Updating Objects ....................... 49
- Deleting Objects .............................................. 50
- Advanced Querying ......................................... 51

- Working with QuerySets ........................................ 52
  - QuerySet Methods ............................................ 52
- Conclusion of Chapter 5 ....................................... 54
- Chapter 6: Django Views and URL Routing ............ 55
  - Understanding Django Views ............................. 55
    - Function-Based Views ..................................... 55
    - Class-Based Views .......................................... 56
    - Rendering Templates ....................................... 57
  - Defining URL Patterns ....................................... 58
    - Basic URL Patterns .......................................... 58
    - Dynamic URL Patterns ..................................... 59
    - Using Regular Expressions .............................. 60
  - Handling Different HTTP Methods ..................... 61
  - Using Django's Generic Views ........................... 62
    - ListView ............................................................. 63
    - DetailView ......................................................... 63
    - Creating Custom Generic Views ...................... 64
  - URL Namespacing ............................................. 65
    - Defining Namespaces ...................................... 65
  - Conclusion of Chapter 6 .................................... 66
- Chapter 7: Django Templates and Template Inheritance ................................................................ 68
  - Creating Templates ........................................... 68

- **Rendering Templates in Views** ............................. 70
- **Template Inheritance** ........................................... 71
  - **Creating a Base Template** .............................. 71
  - **Extending the Base Template** ........................ 73
- **Using Template Tags** ............................................ 74
- **Using Template Filters** ......................................... 75
  - **Common Filters** ............................................... 76
  - **Creating Custom Template Filters** .................. 77
- **Template Context Processors** .............................. 78
  - **Creating a Context Processor** ......................... 78
- **Conclusion of Chapter 7** ....................................... 80
- **Chapter 8: Django Forms and Validation** ............. 82
- **Creating Forms in Django** ..................................... 82
  - **Basic Forms** ..................................................... 82
  - **Using ModelForms** ........................................... 83
- **Rendering Forms in Templates** ............................. 84
- **Handling Form Submissions** ................................. 85
- **Form Validation** ..................................................... 86
  - **Field Validation** ................................................ 87
  - **Form-Wide Validation** ...................................... 88
- **Displaying Validation Errors** .................................. 89
- **Working with Formsets** .......................................... 90
  - **Creating a Formset** .......................................... 91

- Rendering and Handling Formsets ............ 91
- Conclusion of Chapter 8 ........................... 93
- **Chapter 9: Django Models and Database Management** ........................................... 95
  - Defining Models ....................................... 95
    - Creating a Basic Model .......................... 95
    - Field Types ........................................... 97
    - Relationships Between Models ............. 97
  - Database Migrations ................................ 99
    - Creating Migrations ............................... 99
    - Applying Migrations ............................. 100
    - Managing Migrations ........................... 100
  - Using Django's ORM ............................. 101
    - Creating and Saving Instances ............ 102
    - Querying the Database ........................ 102
    - Updating and Deleting Instances ......... 104
  - Customizing Model Behavior ................. 105
    - Model Methods .................................... 105
    - Meta Options ....................................... 106
  - Database Relationships in the Admin Interface 107
    - Inline Models ....................................... 107
  - Conclusion of Chapter 9 ........................ 108

# Chapter 10: Django Admin Interface and Customization .............................................. 109

## Setting Up the Admin Interface ........................... 109

## Registering Models in the Admin ....................... 109

## Customizing the Admin Interface ....................... 109

### Customizing Model Admin Classes ................ 109

### Adding Inline Models ....................................... 109

## Customizing Admin Forms ................................. 109

### Customizing Fieldsets ..................................... 109

### Customizing Widgets ...................................... 109

## Adding Actions in the Admin Interface ............... 109

### Defining Custom Actions ................................. 109

## Customizing the Admin Site ............................... 109

### Changing the Admin Site Header .................... 109

### Styling the Admin Interface ............................. 109

## Implementing Custom Permissions .................... 109

### Custom Permissions on Models ...................... 109

### Restricting Actions Based on Permissions .... 109

## Extending the Admin with Third-Party Packages .............................................................................. 109

### Django Grappelli ............................................... 109

### Django Suit ...................................................... 109

## Conclusion of Chapter 10 .................................... 109

## Chapter 11: Building RESTful APIs with Django Rest Framework .................. 109

### Understanding RESTful APIs ................ 109
#### Key Principles of REST ................ 109
### Setting Up Django Rest Framework ............. 109
### Creating Your First API Endpoint ............. 109
#### Defining a Model ................ 109
#### Creating a Serializer ................ 109
#### Creating API Views ................ 109
#### Configuring URLs ................ 109
### Handling API Requests and Responses ............ 109
#### Retrieving Data ................ 109
#### Creating Data ................ 109
### Implementing Update and Delete Functionality . 109
#### Creating a Detail View ................ 109
#### Configuring URLs for Detail View ............ 109
### Adding Authentication and Permissions .......... 109
#### Authentication Classes ................ 109
#### Configuring Authentication ................ 109
#### Adding Permissions ................ 109
### Handling Pagination ................ 109
#### Configuring Pagination ................ 109
#### Implementing Pagination in Views ............ 109

**Testing Your API** ........................................... 109
  Writing Tests ............................................... 109
**Conclusion of Chapter 11** ............................ 109

**Chapter 12: Flask Fundamentals for Web Development** ................................................. 109

Setting Up Flask............................................. 109
Understanding Flask Routing ....................... 109
  Defining Routes........................................... 109
  Dynamic Routing......................................... 109
Handling Requests and Responses ............. 109
  Accessing Request Data ............................ 109
  Sending Responses .................................... 109
Using Templates with Flask .......................... 109
  Setting Up a Template Directory ................ 109
  Rendering Templates.................................. 109
Working with Forms in Flask ......................... 109
  Creating a Form........................................... 109
  Processing Form Data ................................ 109
Handling Errors and Debugging ................... 109
  Error Handling ............................................. 109
  Debugging.................................................... 109
Structuring a Flask Application..................... 109
  Creating a Package Structure .................... 109

- Initializing the Application ........................... 109
- Integrating with Databases ............................ 109
  - Installing Flask-SQLAlchemy ........................ 109
  - Setting Up SQLAlchemy ............................... 109
  - Defining Models ......................................... 109
  - Creating the Database ................................. 109
- Implementing Middleware in Flask .................. 109
  - Creating Middleware .................................... 109
- Conclusion of Chapter 12 ............................... 109

**Chapter 13: FastAPI for Modern Web Development** ........................................................ 109

- Getting Started with FastAPI .......................... 109
- Understanding FastAPI Routing ..................... 109
  - Defining Routes .......................................... 109
  - Path Parameters and Query Parameters ........ 109
- Handling Requests and Responses ................ 109
  - Request Body Validation ............................. 109
  - Response Models ....................................... 109
- Using Dependency Injection .......................... 109
  - Defining Dependencies ............................... 109
- Handling Errors in FastAPI ............................ 109
  - Custom Exception Handling ........................ 109
- Using Middleware ......................................... 109

- Creating Middleware ......................................... 109
- Implementing Background Tasks ....................... 109
  - Defining Background Tasks............................. 109
- Integrating with Databases ................................ 109
  - Setting Up SQLAlchemy ................................... 109
  - Configuring SQLAlchemy.................................. 109
  - Defining Models................................................ 109
  - Creating the Database ..................................... 109
- Testing Your FastAPI Application ....................... 109
  - Writing Tests .................................................... 109
- Deploying FastAPI Applications ......................... 109
  - Using Uvicorn for Deployment ......................... 109
- Conclusion of Chapter 13 ................................... 109

### Chapter 14: Integrating Django and FastAPI for Scalable Applications ............................................... 109

- Understanding the Integration Architecture ...... 109
  - Microservices vs. Monolithic Architecture ..... 109
  - Communication Between Services ................. 109
- Setting Up the Environment................................ 109
  - Installing Required Packages ......................... 109
  - Creating a Django Project ............................... 109
  - Creating a FastAPI App within Django............ 109
- Routing in Django and FastAPI ........................... 109

    Setting Up Django URLs ................................... 109
    Creating FastAPI Routes ................................. 109
  Managing Shared Resources ........................... 109
    Database Integration ....................................... 109
    Shared Settings and Configuration ................. 109
  Authentication and Security .............................. 109
    Using Django's Authentication System .......... 109
    FastAPI Security Features ............................... 109
  Testing the Integrated Application ...................... 109
    Testing Django Routes .................................... 109
    Testing FastAPI Routes ................................... 109
  Deployment Considerations .............................. 109
    Using ASGI for Deployment ............................ 109
    Using Reverse Proxies .................................... 109
  Conclusion of Chapter 14 ...................................... 109
**Chapter 15: Building a Full-Stack Application with Django and FastAPI** .................................................. 109
  Defining the Application Architecture ................. 109
    Frontend Layer ................................................ 109
    Backend Layer ................................................ 109
    API Layer ......................................................... 109
  Setting Up the Development Environment ......... 109
    Creating the Project Structure ......................... 109

### Installing Django and FastAPI ..........................109
### Creating a Django Project .................................109
### Setting Up FastAPI ............................................109
## Developing the Backend with Django .................109
### Defining Models ...............................................109
### Creating Database Migrations .........................109
### Setting Up the Admin Interface .......................109
### Configuring URLs .............................................109
## Developing the API with FastAPI ........................109
### Setting Up FastAPI Routes ...............................109
### Integrating Django and FastAPI .......................109
## Developing the Frontend with React ..................109
### Creating a React App .......................................109
### Installing Axios for API Calls ............................109
### Creating Components ......................................109
### Rendering the Component ...............................109
### Proxying API Requests ....................................109
## Testing the Full-Stack Application .....................110
### Running the Django and FastAPI Server ........110
### Running the React Development Server ..........110
## Interacting with the Application ..........................110
## Deploying the Full-Stack Application .................110
### Deployment Steps .............................................111

Conclusion of Chapter 15 ..................................... 111

**Chapter 16: API Development Best Practices with FastAPI** ........................................................................ 112

Designing RESTful APIs ...................................... 112

Understanding HTTP Methods .......................... 112

Defining Resource URLs ................................... 112

Versioning Your API .......................................... 113

Structuring Your FastAPI Project ........................ 113

Recommended Directory Structure .................. 113

Organizing Endpoints ....................................... 114

Using Pydantic Models ..................................... 114

Implementing Security ......................................... 114

Using OAuth2 for Authentication ...................... 114

Securing Endpoints .......................................... 115

Validating Data ................................................... 115

Request Validation ........................................... 115

Response Validation ........................................ 115

Optimizing Performance ...................................... 116

Asynchronous Programming ............................ 116

Caching Responses ......................................... 116

Using Background Tasks ................................. 116

Documenting Your API ........................................ 117

Accessing Automatic Documentation ............. 117

- Adding Descriptions and Metadata .................117
- **Testing Your API** ......................................................117
  - Using TestClient ...................................................118
  - Writing Comprehensive Tests ..........................118
- **Conclusion of Chapter 16** .......................................118
- **Chapter 17: Deploying FastAPI Applications in Production** ...................................................................119
- Choosing the Right Hosting Environment .........119
  - Cloud Providers ..................................................119
  - Virtual Private Servers (VPS) .............................119
  - Containerization ..................................................120
- Setting Up the Server ............................................120
  - Installing Required Packages ...........................120
  - Configuring a Virtual Environment...................120
  - Installing FastAPI and Uvicorn .........................120
- Deploying the FastAPI Application .....................121
  - Running Uvicorn .................................................121
  - Using Systemd for Process Management ......121
  - Configuring a Reverse Proxy with Nginx........122
- Managing Dependencies......................................123
  - Creating requirements.txt ................................123
  - Updating Dependencies ...................................123
- Setting Up the Database .......................................123

- Choosing a Database ............................................. 124
- Installing Database Drivers ................................. 124
- Database Configuration ....................................... 124
- Implementing Monitoring and Logging ............... 124
  - Setting Up Logging ............................................. 124
  - Using Monitoring Tools ...................................... 125
  - Error Reporting ................................................... 125
- Ensuring Security Best Practices ........................ 125
  - Using HTTPS ....................................................... 126
  - Environment Variables for Secrets .................. 126
  - Rate Limiting ....................................................... 126
  - Regular Security Audits ..................................... 126
- Testing Your Deployment ....................................... 126
  - Functional Testing .............................................. 126
  - Load Testing ........................................................ 126
- Conclusion of Chapter 17 ...................................... 126

# Chapter 1: Introduction to Python Web Development

Web development is an ever-evolving field, and the demand for skilled developers continues to rise. At the heart of this demand is the need for robust, scalable, and efficient web applications that can serve various purposes—from simple blogs to complex enterprise solutions. Python has emerged as one of the most popular programming languages for web development due to its readability, versatility, and the powerful frameworks it offers. This chapter will explore the fundamentals of web development, the role of Python, and the significance of popular frameworks like Django, Flask, and FastAPI.

## Understanding Web Development

Web development encompasses the tasks associated with developing websites for hosting via intranet or the internet. It includes aspects such as web design, web content development, client-side/server-side scripting, and network security configuration. The landscape of web development can generally be divided into two main areas: front-end and back-end development.

Front-end development focuses on the visual elements of a website—the parts users interact with directly. This includes everything from layout and design to interactivity and user experience. Technologies such as HTML, CSS, and JavaScript are the cornerstones of front-end development, allowing developers to create visually appealing and responsive user interfaces.

In contrast, back-end development deals with the server side of a web application. This involves managing databases, server logic, authentication, and the integration of various services. Back-end developers often work with languages like Python, Ruby, PHP, and Java, utilizing frameworks that simplify the development process and enhance productivity.

# The Role of Python in Web Development

Python has gained immense popularity in recent years, particularly in web development. Its syntax is clear and straightforward, making it an excellent choice for beginners and seasoned developers alike. The language supports multiple programming paradigms, including procedural, object-oriented, and functional programming, which allows developers to choose the best approach for their projects.

One of the key advantages of Python is its vast ecosystem of libraries and frameworks. These tools facilitate rapid development and deployment, allowing developers to focus on building unique features rather than reinventing the wheel. Python frameworks such as Django, Flask, and FastAPI streamline the development process, providing essential functionalities out of the box.

# Exploring Popular Python Frameworks

## Django: The High-Level Framework

Django is a high-level web framework that encourages rapid development and clean, pragmatic design. It follows the "batteries-included" philosophy, meaning it comes with a plethora of built-in features, such as an ORM (Object-Relational Mapping) system, an authentication system, and an admin panel. This makes it an ideal choice for developers who need to build robust applications quickly.

Django is particularly well-suited for larger applications where scalability and maintainability are paramount. Its structure promotes best practices, ensuring that developers can create code that is easy to read and manage. With a vibrant community and extensive documentation, Django provides ample resources for developers of all skill levels.

## Flask: The Lightweight Framework

In contrast to Django, Flask is a micro-framework that is lightweight and flexible. It provides the essentials needed to get a web application up and running, while allowing developers the freedom to choose how they want to structure their applications. Flask is highly modular, which means you can easily add extensions to enhance its functionality.

Flask is perfect for smaller applications or projects where speed and simplicity are key. Its minimalistic design allows for quick iterations and is particularly attractive to developers who prefer a hands-on approach. Flask's ease of use makes it a popular choice for prototyping and building RESTful APIs.

### FastAPI: The Modern Framework

FastAPI is a relatively new framework that has gained traction due to its focus on high performance and ease of use. Built on top of Starlette and Pydantic, FastAPI allows developers to create APIs with automatic generation of interactive documentation. Its asynchronous capabilities enable the development of applications that can handle many requests simultaneously, making it ideal for high-load environments.

FastAPI emphasizes type hinting, which enhances code clarity and allows for more robust validation of input data. This makes it easier to catch errors early in the development process and improves the overall quality of the code. FastAPI is particularly well-suited for building microservices and modern web applications that require speed and efficiency.

# The Importance of Frameworks

Frameworks play a crucial role in web development. They provide developers with the structure and tools needed to build applications efficiently. By utilizing frameworks, developers can adhere to industry best practices, enhance maintainability, and reduce the risk of common pitfalls associated with web development.

Using a framework allows developers to focus on building unique features rather than dealing with low-level details. This leads to faster development cycles and helps teams deliver products more quickly. Furthermore, frameworks often come with built-in security features, which help protect applications from common vulnerabilities.

## Conclusion of Chapter 1

The landscape of web development is vast, and Python stands out as a powerful tool for building dynamic, high-quality web applications. Understanding the distinctions between front-end and back-end development, along with the importance of frameworks, sets the stage for exploring more advanced topics in subsequent chapters. As we delve into Django, Flask, and FastAPI, you will gain hands-on experience and insights into creating robust web applications tailored to your specific needs.

This foundation will empower you to make informed choices as you embark on your journey into Python web development, equipped with the knowledge of best practices and the tools necessary for success.

# Chapter 2: Setting Up Your Development Environment

Setting up a proper development environment is crucial for any web development project. A well-organized environment allows developers to work efficiently, minimize errors, and streamline collaboration. This chapter will guide you through the essential steps to establish your Python web development environment, including installing Python, managing packages, and choosing the right tools for your workflow.

## Installing Python

Before diving into web development, the first step is to ensure that Python is installed on your machine. Python can be downloaded from the official Python website, where you'll find versions for Windows, macOS, and Linux. It's important to choose the latest stable version to take advantage of the newest features and optimizations.

Once the installer is downloaded, you can proceed with the installation. On Windows, make sure to check the box that adds Python to your system PATH, which simplifies running Python from the command line. On macOS and Linux, you can often use package managers like Homebrew or apt-get for easy installation.

After installation, you can verify that Python is installed correctly by opening your terminal or command prompt and typing `python --version` or `python3 --version`. This command should display the installed version of Python, confirming that the installation was successful.

# Creating and Managing Virtual Environments

Managing dependencies is a critical part of web development, especially as projects grow in size and complexity. This is where virtual environments come into play. A virtual environment allows you to create isolated spaces for your projects, ensuring that dependencies don't conflict with each other.

To create a virtual environment, you can use the built-in `venv` module. Navigate to your project directory in the terminal and run the command `python -m venv env`. This command creates a directory named `env` containing the virtual environment. To activate it, you'll use different commands depending on your operating system:

- **On Windows:** .\env\Scripts\activate
- **On macOS/Linux:** source env/bin/activate

Once activated, you'll notice the terminal prompt changes to indicate that you are now working within the virtual environment. From here, you can install packages using pip without affecting your global Python installation.

To deactivate the virtual environment, simply run the command deactivate. It's a good practice to create a new virtual environment for each project to keep dependencies organized and manageable.

## Managing Packages with pip

Python's package manager, pip, is an essential tool for installing and managing external libraries and frameworks. With pip, you can easily add functionality to your projects, such as database integration, web frameworks, and utility libraries.

To install a package, you can use the command pip install package_name. For instance, to install Django, you would run pip install Django. If you need to install a specific version, you can specify it like this: `pip install Django==3.2.5`.

It's also important to keep track of your project's dependencies. A common practice is to create a `requirements.txt` file that lists all the packages your project needs. You can generate this file automatically with the command `pip freeze > requirements.txt`. This file can then be shared with others or used to replicate the environment by running `pip install -r requirements.txt`.

# Choosing an Integrated Development Environment (IDE)

Selecting the right IDE or code editor is crucial for enhancing productivity and streamlining the development process. An IDE typically offers features such as syntax highlighting, debugging tools, and integration with version control systems. Some popular choices for Python web development include:

Visual Studio Code (VS Code) is a highly versatile and popular code editor that supports numerous extensions. With its rich ecosystem, developers can customize it to fit their workflow perfectly. Features like integrated terminal and debugging tools make it an ideal choice for web development.

PyCharm, developed by JetBrains, is a powerful IDE specifically designed for Python. It comes with advanced features like intelligent code completion, project navigation, and a built-in terminal. The professional edition offers additional support for web frameworks, making it a robust option for Django, Flask, and FastAPI development.

Sublime Text is a lightweight code editor that is fast and efficient. While it lacks some advanced features of an IDE, its simplicity and speed make it a favorite among developers. With various plugins available, it can be tailored to fit different development needs.

Choosing an IDE is often a matter of personal preference, so it's worthwhile to experiment with a few to see which one best suits your workflow.

## Version Control with Git

Version control is an essential aspect of software development that allows you to track changes, collaborate with others, and manage code effectively. Git is the most widely used version control system, enabling developers to maintain a history of their project and revert to previous versions if needed.

To start using Git, you'll need to install it on your machine. You can download it from the official Git website or use a package manager. Once installed, you can initialize a Git repository in your project directory by running the command `git init`. This command sets up a `.git` directory that will track changes.

When making changes, you can stage them for commit with `git add .` and commit them with `git commit -m "Your commit message"`. It's essential to write meaningful commit messages that describe the changes made.

If you plan to collaborate with others, you can host your Git repository on platforms like GitHub, GitLab, or Bitbucket. These platforms provide additional features for code review, issue tracking, and project management, making it easier to work in teams.

## Setting Up a Local Web Server

Once your development environment is configured, you'll need to set up a local web server to test your applications. Both Django and Flask come with built-in development servers that can be easily launched.

In Django, you can start the development server with the command python manage.py runserver. By default, it will run on localhost:8000. You can access your application by navigating to http://127.0.0.1:8000 in your web browser.

Flask's development server can be started with flask run. You may need to set the FLASK_APP environment variable to your main application file. The server will typically run on localhost:5000.

Using a local web server allows you to test your application in a controlled environment, ensuring everything functions as intended before deployment.

## Conclusion of Chapter 2

Establishing a well-configured development environment is the backbone of successful web development. By installing Python, creating virtual environments, managing packages, and selecting the right tools, you can create a productive workspace tailored to your needs. With version control and local web servers in place, you'll be well-prepared to start building robust web applications. As you move forward, these foundational skills will enable you to navigate the complexities of web development with confidence.

# Chapter 3: Introduction to Django

Django is one of the most popular web frameworks in the Python ecosystem, renowned for its "batteries-included" approach that simplifies the development of robust web applications. This chapter will provide an in-depth exploration of Django, covering its architecture, key features, and the philosophy behind its design. Additionally, we will touch on its ecosystem and the community that surrounds it, which contributes to its ongoing evolution and adoption.

## What is Django?

Django is an open-source web framework written in Python that facilitates the development of secure and maintainable web applications. Originally created by a group of developers at a newspaper company, Django was designed to address the challenges of building complex web applications quickly and efficiently. It emphasizes the reusability of components, rapid development, and the principle of "don't repeat yourself" (DRY).

Django follows the Model-View-Template (MVT) architectural pattern, which separates the application logic, presentation layer, and data management. This separation helps developers maintain clean and organized code, making it easier to collaborate and scale applications.

# Key Features of Django

## 1. ORM (Object-Relational Mapping)

One of Django's standout features is its built-in ORM, which allows developers to interact with databases using Python objects instead of SQL queries. The ORM abstracts the complexities of database management, enabling developers to define their data models as Python classes. These classes translate into database tables, making it easy to perform CRUD (Create, Read, Update, Delete) operations.

Django's ORM supports various database backends, including PostgreSQL, MySQL, SQLite, and Oracle. This flexibility allows developers to choose the database that best fits their project requirements.

## 2. Admin Interface

Django includes a powerful and customizable admin interface out of the box. This feature allows developers to manage application data, user permissions, and content without the need to create a separate interface. The admin panel is automatically generated based on the defined models, providing a user-friendly way to interact with the application's data.

The admin interface is highly customizable, allowing developers to tailor its appearance and functionality according to specific needs. This is especially useful for content management systems (CMS) or applications with complex data structures.

## 3. Authentication and Authorization

Django comes with a robust authentication and authorization system that simplifies user management. It includes features such as user registration, login/logout, password management, and user permissions. This built-in functionality allows developers to implement security best practices without starting from scratch.

Django's authentication system can be easily extended, enabling developers to customize user models and implement additional features like two-factor authentication or social authentication using third-party providers.

## 4. URL Routing

Django's URL routing system is both flexible and powerful. It allows developers to define clean, readable URLs for their applications, which can enhance SEO and user experience. Developers can use regular expressions to create dynamic URLs that capture variables, making it easy to create RESTful APIs.

The routing system supports URL namespaces, allowing developers to group related views and URLs, which is particularly useful for larger applications.

## 5. Middleware Support

Middleware in Django is a way to process requests globally before they reach the view or after the view has processed them. Django includes several built-in middleware components for handling sessions, user authentication, cross-site request forgery protection, and more.

Custom middleware can also be created, allowing developers to implement additional processing steps for requests and responses, such as logging, modifying request data, or managing cross-origin resource sharing (CORS).

## 6. Security Features

Django takes security seriously and provides several built-in features to help developers protect their applications from common vulnerabilities. These include protection against SQL injection, cross-site scripting (XSS), cross-site request forgery (CSRF), and clickjacking.

Django encourages best practices by enforcing the use of secure passwords and HTTPS. Additionally, it includes features for handling user sessions securely.

## 7. Scalability and Performance

Django is designed to scale, making it suitable for projects of varying sizes. The framework supports horizontal scaling, allowing applications to handle increased traffic by distributing requests across multiple servers.

Django's caching framework further enhances performance by enabling developers to cache pages or data at different levels, such as the view level, template level, or database query level. This capability significantly reduces the load on the server and improves response times.

# Django's Architecture: The MVT Pattern

Django's architecture follows the Model-View-Template (MVT) pattern, which is similar to the more commonly known Model-View-Controller (MVC) pattern. Understanding how these components interact is essential for effectively using Django.

### Model

The Model represents the data structure of the application. In Django, models are defined as Python classes that inherit from django.db.models.Model. Each model class corresponds to a database table, and the class attributes represent the table fields. The ORM allows developers to perform database operations without writing raw SQL, making data manipulation straightforward.

### View

The View is responsible for processing user requests and returning appropriate responses. In Django, views are defined as Python functions or classes that take a web request and return a web response. Views can render HTML templates, return JSON data, or redirect users to other pages. Django encourages developers to keep business logic within views, while delegating presentation logic to templates.

### Template

Templates are the presentation layer of a Django application. They define how data is presented to users. Django uses its own templating language, which allows developers to embed Python-like expressions within HTML. Templates can inherit from one another, making it easy to create reusable components and maintain consistency across the application.

# The Philosophy of Django

Django is built on a set of guiding principles that aim to make web development easier and more efficient. These principles include:

- **Reusability**: Django encourages developers to create reusable components, which can be easily shared across projects. This philosophy promotes code quality and reduces redundancy.
- **Rapid Development**: With its rich set of built-in features, Django enables developers to build applications quickly without sacrificing quality. This rapid development cycle is particularly beneficial for startups and small teams.
- **Secure by Default**: Django's built-in security features help developers follow best practices and protect their applications from vulnerabilities. This focus on security is essential in today's web landscape.

# Django's Ecosystem and Community

The Django ecosystem is vast, comprising numerous third-party packages and libraries that extend its functionality. Popular packages include Django REST framework for building APIs, Celery for handling background tasks, and Django Channels for real-time applications. These packages enhance Django's capabilities, making it suitable for a wide range of projects.

The Django community is vibrant and supportive, offering numerous resources for developers. Official documentation is comprehensive, covering everything from basic concepts to advanced topics. Additionally, there are countless tutorials, forums, and user groups where developers can seek help and share knowledge.

Django also hosts an annual conference known as DjangoCon, bringing together developers to discuss best practices, share projects, and network. This community-driven approach ensures that Django remains up-to-date with modern web development trends and continues to evolve.

## Conclusion of Chapter 3

Django is a powerful framework that streamlines the development of secure and maintainable web applications. Its rich feature set, adherence to best practices, and strong community support make it a compelling choice for developers. In the following chapters, we will delve deeper into building applications with Django, exploring its various components and capabilities to create robust web solutions.

# Chapter 4: Setting Up a Django Project

Setting up a Django project is the first step toward building robust web applications. This chapter will guide you through the process of creating a new Django project from scratch, configuring essential settings, and understanding the directory structure that Django generates. By the end of this chapter, you'll be equipped to create and manage your own Django projects effectively.

## Creating a New Django Project

To start a new Django project, you first need to ensure that Django is installed in your virtual environment. If you haven't installed Django yet, you can do so by activating your virtual environment and running the command pip install django. Once Django is installed, you can create a new project using the django-admin command.

Open your terminal and navigate to the directory where you want to create your project. Use the following command to create a new Django project, replacing myproject with your desired project name:

```bash
Copy code
django-admin startproject myproject
```

This command creates a new directory named `myproject` containing the essential files and subdirectories required for a Django project.

## Understanding the Project Structure

After running the `startproject` command, you will see the following directory structure:

```markdown
Copy code
myproject/
    manage.py
    myproject/
        __init__.py
        settings.py
        urls.py
        asgi.py
        wsgi.py
```

**1. `manage.py`**

The manage.py file is a command-line utility that allows you to interact with your Django project. You can use it to run the development server, create new apps, apply database migrations, and more. For example, to run the development server, you would use the command:

bash
Copy code
```
python manage.py runserver
```

This command starts the server and makes your application accessible at http://127.0.0.1:8000.

## 2. settings.py

The settings.py file contains all the configuration options for your Django project. This includes database settings, installed apps, middleware, and static files configurations. Each of these settings plays a critical role in how your application behaves.

For example, you will define your database engine, name, and connection details in this file. By default, Django is set up to use SQLite, but you can easily switch to other databases such as PostgreSQL or MySQL.

### 3. urls.py

The urls.py file is where you define the URL patterns for your application. Django uses these patterns to route incoming requests to the appropriate view functions. Initially, this file contains a basic URL configuration, but as you develop your application, you will add more patterns to accommodate various views.

### 4. asgi.py and wsgi.py

These files are entry points for your application when deploying it using ASGI (Asynchronous Server Gateway Interface) or WSGI (Web Server Gateway Interface). While you won't need to modify these files often, they are essential for deploying your application on production servers.

### 5. __init__.py

This empty file signifies that the directory should be treated as a Python package. It allows you to import modules from the project folder and is necessary for Python's module system to recognize the directory.

## Configuring Settings

Once your project is created, the next step is to configure your settings. Open the settings.py file to begin customizing your project. Here are some key settings you should pay attention to:

## 1. Database Configuration

By default, Django uses SQLite, which is great for development but not suitable for production. To switch to another database, you'll need to modify the DATABASES setting. For example, to use PostgreSQL, you would update it as follows:

python
Copy code
```
DATABASES = {
   'default': {
      'ENGINE': 'django.db.backends.postgresql',
      'NAME': 'mydatabase',
      'USER': 'myuser',
      'PASSWORD': 'mypassword',
      'HOST': 'localhost',
      'PORT': '',
   }
}
```

Make sure to install the necessary database adapter, such as psycopg2 for PostgreSQL, using pip.

## 2. Allowed Hosts

The ALLOWED_HOSTS setting is a security measure that defines which hosts are allowed to serve your Django application. For local development, you can set it to:

python
Copy code
ALLOWED_HOSTS = ['localhost', '127.0.0.1']

For production, you will need to specify your domain names.

## 3. Static and Media Files

Django manages static files (CSS, JavaScript, images) and media files (user-uploaded content) separately. You'll need to set the paths for these files in the settings:

python
Copy code
STATIC_URL = '/static/'

STATIC_ROOT = BASE_DIR / 'staticfiles'

MEDIA_URL = '/media/'
MEDIA_ROOT = BASE_DIR / 'media'

Make sure to create corresponding directories to hold these files.

## 4. Installed Apps

The INSTALLED_APPS setting is a list of applications that are active in your Django project. This list includes both Django's built-in apps and any custom apps you create. For example:

python
Copy code
```
INSTALLED_APPS = [
    'django.contrib.admin',
    'django.contrib.auth',
    'django.contrib.contenttypes',
    'django.contrib.sessions',
    'django.contrib.messages',
    'django.contrib.staticfiles',
    'myapp',  # Your custom app
]
```

You will add your custom apps here as you create them.

## Creating a Django App

In Django, an application is a web component that performs a specific task. For example, a blog, a forum, or a user authentication system can all be considered separate applications. To create a new app within your project, use the manage.py command:

bash
Copy code
```
python manage.py startapp myapp
```

This command creates a new directory named myapp with a structure similar to this:

markdown
Copy code
```
myapp/
    migrations/
        __init__.py
    __init__.py
    admin.py
    apps.py
```

models.py
tests.py
views.py

## 1. models.py

The models.py file is where you define your data models. Each model corresponds to a database table and is defined as a Python class that inherits from django.db.models.Model. For example:

python
Copy code
```
from django.db import models

class Post(models.Model):
    title = models.CharField(max_length=200)
    content = models.TextField()
    created_at = models.DateTimeField(auto_now_add=True)
```

## 2. views.py

The views.py file contains the view functions that handle requests and return responses. For example, you can define a view that retrieves all blog posts and renders them in a template:

```python
Copy code
from django.shortcuts import render
from .models import Post

def post_list(request):
    posts = Post.objects.all()
    return render(request, 'myapp/post_list.html', {'posts': posts})
```

### 3. admin.py

In the admin.py file, you can register your models with the Django admin interface. This allows you to manage your application's data through the admin panel easily:

```python
Copy code
from django.contrib import admin
from .models import Post

admin.site.register(Post)
```

# Running the Development Server

After creating your app and configuring your settings, it's time to see your application in action. Make sure to run migrations to create the necessary database tables:

bash
Copy code
```
python manage.py migrate
```

This command applies any pending migrations, setting up the initial database structure. Next, you can start the development server:

bash
Copy code
```
python manage.py runserver
```

Navigate to http://127.0.0.1:8000 in your web browser, and you should see the default Django welcome page. This indicates that your project is up and running.

# Conclusion of Chapter 4

Setting up a Django project involves creating the project structure, configuring settings, and creating applications. Understanding the components of your project, such as models, views, and templates, is crucial for building scalable web applications. With your project set up and the development server running, you are now ready to delve deeper into the intricacies of Django and start developing your web application.

# Chapter 5: Django Models and the ORM

Django's powerful Object-Relational Mapping (ORM) system is one of its standout features, enabling developers to interact with databases using Python classes instead of SQL queries. This chapter will provide an in-depth exploration of Django models, the ORM, and how to effectively create, manage, and query your data.

## Understanding Django Models

Django models are Python classes that represent database tables. Each model corresponds to a single table, and each attribute of the model represents a column in that table. By defining models, you can easily create, retrieve, update, and delete records in your database.

### Creating a Model

To create a model in Django, you define a Python class that inherits from django.db.models.Model. Each class attribute represents a field in the database. For example, consider a simple blog application where you want to store posts. You might create a model like this:

python
Copy code
```
from django.db import models

class Post(models.Model):
    title = models.CharField(max_length=200)
    content = models.TextField()
    created_at = models.DateTimeField(auto_now_add=True)
    updated_at = models.DateTimeField(auto_now=True)

    def __str__(self):
        return self.title
```

In this example, the Post model has four fields: title, content, created_at, and updated_at. The CharField and TextField types are commonly used for string data, while DateTimeField is useful for timestamps. The __str__ method returns a string representation of the model instance, which is particularly useful in the Django admin interface.

## Field Types

Django provides a rich set of field types that allow you to define the kind of data that can be stored. Some common field types include:

- CharField: A string field for short text, requires a max_length argument.
- TextField: A large text field for longer content, without a maximum length.
- IntegerField: A field for storing integers.
- FloatField: A field for storing floating-point numbers.
- BooleanField: A field for storing boolean values.
- DateTimeField: A field for storing date and time values.
- EmailField: A field for storing email addresses, with built-in validation.

By leveraging these field types, you can effectively model the data structure of your application.

## Defining Relationships

Django models also allow you to define relationships between different models. The primary types of relationships are:

- **One-to-One Relationship**: This is established using OneToOneField. For instance, if you want to create a user profile linked to the Django user model, you would use:

python
Copy code
```
from django.contrib.auth.models import User

class Profile(models.Model):
    user = models.OneToOneField(User, on_delete=models.CASCADE)
    bio = models.TextField()
```

- **One-to-Many Relationship**: This is established using ForeignKey. For example, if each post can have multiple comments, you would define it like this:

python
Copy code
```
class Comment(models.Model):
    post = models.ForeignKey(Post, on_delete=models.CASCADE)
    content = models.TextField()
```

- **Many-to-Many Relationship**: This is established using ManyToManyField. For instance, if a post can have multiple tags, and each tag can be associated with multiple posts, you would use:

python
Copy code
```
class Tag(models.Model):
    name = models.CharField(max_length=50)

class Post(models.Model):
    tags = models.ManyToManyField(Tag)
```

These relationships allow you to structure your data efficiently, enabling complex queries and interactions between models.

# Database Migrations

After defining your models, the next step is to create the corresponding database tables. Django uses a system called migrations to manage changes to the database schema.

### Creating Migrations

To create a migration for your models, you run the following command:

bash
Copy code
```
python manage.py makemigrations
```

This command analyzes your models and generates migration files that describe the changes required to create the corresponding database tables. These migration files are stored in the migrations directory within your app.

## Applying Migrations

To apply the migrations and create the database tables, you use:

bash
Copy code
```
python manage.py migrate
```

This command executes the SQL commands generated by the migrations, ensuring your database schema is in sync with your models. Migrations can also be used to update existing tables, making it easy to manage changes over time.

# Querying the Database with the ORM

Django's ORM allows you to perform database queries using Python code. This abstraction eliminates the need for writing raw SQL, making your code more readable and maintainable.

## Retrieving Objects

To retrieve objects from the database, you can use the Model.objects manager, which provides a rich API for querying. Here are some common methods:

- **All Objects**: To retrieve all objects of a model:

python
Copy code
```
posts = Post.objects.all()
```

- **Filter Objects**: To filter objects based on specific criteria:

python
Copy code
```
recent_posts = Post.objects.filter(created_at__gte='2024-01-01')
```

- **Get a Single Object**: To retrieve a single object that matches a condition:

python
Copy code
```
try:
    post = Post.objects.get(id=1)
except Post.DoesNotExist:
    post = None
```

## Creating and Updating Objects

You can create new objects and save them to the database easily:

python
Copy code
```
new_post = Post(title='My First Post', content='This is the content of my first post.')
new_post.save()
```

To update an existing object, retrieve it and modify its attributes:

python
Copy code

```python
post = Post.objects.get(id=1)
post.title = 'Updated Title'
post.save()
```

## Deleting Objects

To delete objects from the database, you can use the delete() method:

python
Copy code
```python
post = Post.objects.get(id=1)
post.delete()
```

This method will remove the object from the database permanently.

## Advanced Querying

Django's ORM supports advanced querying techniques, allowing you to perform complex operations with ease. You can chain filters, order results, and even aggregate data.

- **Chaining Filters**: You can chain multiple filter conditions:

python

Copy code
```
posts = Post.objects.filter(created_at__gte='2024-01-01').order_by('-created_at')
```

- **Aggregations**: To perform aggregations, you can use functions from django.db.models:

python
Copy code
```
from django.db.models import Count

post_count = Post.objects.aggregate(total_posts=Count('id'))
```

# Working with QuerySets

Django's ORM queries return a QuerySet, which is a collection of database results. QuerySets are lazy, meaning they don't hit the database until they are explicitly evaluated. This allows you to build complex queries without executing unnecessary database operations.

### QuerySet Methods

Some useful methods for working with QuerySets include:

- **count()**: Returns the number of objects in the QuerySet.

python
Copy code
```
total_posts = Post.objects.count()
```

- **exists()**: Checks if any objects match the query.

python
Copy code
```
if Post.objects.filter(title='My First Post').exists():
    print("Post exists!")
```

- **first() and last()**: Retrieve the first or last object from the QuerySet.

python
Copy code
```
first_post = Post.objects.first()
last_post = Post.objects.last()
```

- **distinct()**: Returns only unique results.

python
Copy code

```python
unique_tags = Tag.objects.distinct()
```

By utilizing these QuerySet methods, you can manipulate and analyze your data effectively.

## Conclusion of Chapter 5

Django's ORM and model system provide a powerful way to define and interact with your application's data. By creating models, managing migrations, and leveraging the ORM for querying, you can develop data-driven applications efficiently. Understanding how to work with models and the ORM is essential for building robust Django applications that can scale and evolve over time.

# Chapter 6: Django Views and URL Routing

In Django, views and URL routing form the backbone of your web application's interaction with users. Views define the logic behind handling requests and returning responses, while URL routing maps URLs to specific views. This chapter will explore how to create views, define URL patterns, and handle different types of requests, enabling you to build dynamic web applications.

## Understanding Django Views

A view in Django is a Python function or class that takes a web request and returns a web response. This response can be an HTML page, JSON data, or any other type of content. Views encapsulate the logic required to process user input and generate the appropriate output.

### Function-Based Views

The simplest way to define a view is through a function-based view (FBV). Here's a basic example of a function-based view that returns a simple HTML response:

python
Copy code
```
from django.http import HttpResponse

def home(request):
    return HttpResponse("Welcome to my website!")
```

In this example, the home function takes a request object and returns an HttpResponse with a welcome message. You can easily extend this to render templates or process data.

## Class-Based Views

Django also supports class-based views (CBVs), which provide a more organized and reusable way to define views. Class-based views are particularly useful when you need to handle multiple HTTP methods or share common functionality among views. Here's an example of a class-based view:

python
Copy code
```
from django.views import View
from django.http import HttpResponse
```

```python
class HomeView(View):
    def get(self, request):
        return HttpResponse("Welcome to my website!")
```

In this example, the HomeView class inherits from View, and the get method handles GET requests. You can define additional methods for handling other HTTP methods like POST, PUT, or DELETE.

## Rendering Templates

To return more complex responses, you'll often want to render HTML templates. Django provides a templating engine that allows you to create dynamic HTML pages. Here's how you can modify the function-based view to render a template:

python
Copy code
```python
from django.shortcuts import render

def home(request):
    return render(request, 'home.html', {'title': 'Home Page'})
```

In this example, the render function takes the request, the name of the template file, and a context dictionary containing any data you want to pass to the template. The template can then use this data to generate dynamic content.

## Defining URL Patterns

URL routing in Django is managed through a URL configuration file, typically named urls.py. This file maps URL patterns to specific views, allowing Django to determine which view to invoke based on the incoming request.

### Basic URL Patterns

Here's an example of a simple URL configuration:

```python
Copy code
from django.urls import path
from .views import home

urlpatterns = [
    path('', home, name='home'),
]
```

In this example, the urlpatterns list contains a single URL pattern that maps the root URL ('') to the home view. The name argument provides a name for the URL pattern, which can be useful for reverse URL resolution.

## Dynamic URL Patterns

You can also create dynamic URL patterns that capture parameters from the URL. For instance, if you want to create a blog post detail view that takes a post ID, you could define the URL pattern like this:

python
Copy code
```
from django.urls import path
from .views import post_detail

urlpatterns = [
    path('post/<int:id>/', post_detail, name='post_detail'),
]
```

In this example, <int:id> captures an integer from the URL and passes it as an argument to the post_detail view.

## Using Regular Expressions

For more complex URL patterns, you can use regular expressions. Django provides the `re_path` function for this purpose:

python
Copy code
```
from django.urls import re_path
from .views import post_detail

urlpatterns = [
    re_path(r'^post/(?P<id>\d+)/$', post_detail, name='post_detail'),
]
```

This pattern captures the post ID using a named group (`(?P<id>\d+)`), allowing you to retrieve it in the view.

# Handling Different HTTP Methods

Django views can handle different HTTP methods, such as GET, POST, PUT, and DELETE. This is especially useful for web forms and API endpoints. In function-based views, you can check the request method and respond accordingly:

python

Copy code
```python
from django.http import JsonResponse

def post_detail(request, id):
    if request.method == 'GET':
        # Logic to retrieve the post
        return JsonResponse({'post_id': id})
    elif request.method == 'POST':
        # Logic to create a new post
        return JsonResponse({'message': 'Post created!'})
```

In class-based views, you can define separate methods for each HTTP method:

python
Copy code
```python
class PostDetailView(View):
    def get(self, request, id):
        # Logic to retrieve the post
        return JsonResponse({'post_id': id})

    def post(self, request, id):
        # Logic to create a new post
        return JsonResponse({'message': 'Post created!'})
```

This separation of logic helps keep your code organized and maintainable.

# Using Django's Generic Views

Django provides a set of built-in generic views that handle common patterns, such as displaying a list of objects or a detail view for a single object. These generic views can save you time and reduce code duplication.

## ListView

The ListView is a generic view for displaying a list of objects. Here's an example of how to use it:

python
Copy code
```
from django.views.generic import ListView
from .models import Post

class PostListView(ListView):
    model = Post
    template_name = 'post_list.html'
    context_object_name = 'posts'
```

In this example, PostListView automatically retrieves all Post objects from the database and renders them using the specified template.

## DetailView

The DetailView is used for displaying a single object. Here's how to implement it:

python
Copy code
```
from django.views.generic import DetailView

class PostDetailView(DetailView):
    model = Post
    template_name = 'post_detail.html'
    context_object_name = 'post'
```

This class automatically handles retrieving the specific Post instance based on the URL parameter and rendering the detail template.

## Creating Custom Generic Views

You can also extend the functionality of generic views by overriding methods or adding custom behavior. For example, you might want to add additional context data to your views:

python
Copy code
```
class PostListView(ListView):
    model = Post
    template_name = 'post_list.html'
```

```python
    context_object_name = 'posts'

    def get_context_data(self, **kwargs):
        context = super().get_context_data(**kwargs)
        context['extra_data'] = 'This is additional context'
        return context
```

# URL Namespacing

In larger projects with multiple apps, you might encounter URL name collisions. To avoid this, you can use URL namespacing. This involves defining a namespace for your app's URLs, allowing you to reference them uniquely.

## Defining Namespaces

When including an app's URLs in the project's main urls.py, you can define a namespace like this:

python
Copy code
```
from django.urls import include, path

urlpatterns = [
    path('blog/', include(('blog.urls', 'blog'), namespace='blog')),
```

]

In this example, any URLs defined in the blog app will be namespaced under blog. You can then reference them in your templates or views using the namespace:

html
Copy code
```
<a href="{% url 'blog:post_detail' id=post.id %}">View Post</a>
```

## Conclusion of Chapter 6

Django views and URL routing are essential components of web application development. Understanding how to define views, handle requests, and manage URL patterns allows you to create dynamic, user-friendly applications. With the ability to leverage function-based and class-based views, as well as Django's generic views, you can streamline your development process and build maintainable code structures. This foundational knowledge prepares you for more advanced topics in the following chapters.

# Chapter 7: Django Templates and Template Inheritance

Django's templating system is a powerful feature that allows developers to create dynamic and reusable HTML structures. Templates separate the presentation layer from the business logic, making it easier to manage and maintain web applications. This chapter explores how to create and use templates, implement template inheritance, and utilize template tags and filters to enhance your web pages.

## Creating Templates

Templates in Django are plain HTML files enhanced with Django's template language. This language allows you to incorporate dynamic data and control structures into your HTML. To create a template, you typically place your HTML files in a templates directory within your Django app.

For example, let's create a basic template for a blog post listing. In your app's templates directory, create a file named post_list.html:

html
Copy code
```html
<!DOCTYPE html>
<html lang="en">
<head>
   <meta charset="UTF-8">
   <meta name="viewport" content="width=device-width, initial-scale=1.0">
   <title>Blog Posts</title>
</head>
<body>
   <h1>Blog Posts</h1>
   <ul>
      {% for post in posts %}
         <li>{{ post.title }}</li>
      {% empty %}
         <li>No posts available.</li>
      {% endfor %}
   </ul>
</body>
</html>
```

In this example, the template uses the {% for %} tag to iterate over a list of posts and render their titles. The `{% empty %}` tag provides a fallback in case the list is empty.

## Rendering Templates in Views

To render templates, you typically use the `render` function in your views. Here's how to modify your `PostListView` to render the `post_list.html` template:

python
Copy code
```
from django.views.generic import ListView
from .models import Post
from django.shortcuts import render

class PostListView(ListView):
    model = Post
    template_name = 'post_list.html'
    context_object_name = 'posts'
```

In this case, `ListView` automatically provides a context variable named `posts`, which contains all the `Post` objects retrieved from the database. The specified template will display these posts.

## Template Inheritance

One of the most powerful features of Django's templating system is template inheritance, which allows you to create a base template and extend it in child templates. This approach promotes code reuse and consistency across your application.

## Creating a Base Template

First, create a base template named base.html:

html
Copy code
```
<!DOCTYPE html>
<html lang="en">
<head>
  <meta charset="UTF-8">
  <meta name="viewport" content="width=device-width, initial-scale=1.0">
  <title>{% block title %}My Blog{% endblock %}</title>
</head>
<body>
  <header>
    <h1>My Blog</h1>
    <nav>
      <ul>
        <li><a href="{% url 'home' %}">Home</a></li>
```

```html
        <li><a href="{% url 'post_list' %}">Posts</a></li>
      </ul>
    </nav>
  </header>

  <main>
    {% block content %}
    {% endblock %}
  </main>

  <footer>
    <p>© 2024 My Blog. All rights reserved.</p>
  </footer>
</body>
</html>
```

In this base template, the `{% block %}` tags define areas where child templates can insert content. The `title` block is used for the page title, while the `content` block is where the main body of the page will go.

## Extending the Base Template

Now, modify the `post_list.html` to extend the `base.html` template:

html

**Copy code**
```
{% extends 'base.html' %}

{% block title %}Blog Posts{% endblock %}

{% block content %}
  <h2>Blog Posts</h2>
  <ul>
    {% for post in posts %}
      <li>{{ post.title }}</li>
    {% empty %}
      <li>No posts available.</li>
    {% endfor %}
  </ul>
{% endblock %}
```

By using the `{% extends %}` tag, this template inherits the structure from base.html. The content defined in the `content` block replaces the corresponding block in the base template.

## Using Template Tags

Django templates support a variety of built-in template tags that allow you to control the flow of your template logic and manipulate data. Some common template tags include:

- **Control Structures**: Tags like {% if %}, {% for %}, and {% with %} help you manage conditional logic and loops.

html
Copy code
```
{% if user.is_authenticated %}
    <p>Welcome, {{ user.username }}!</p>
{% else %}
    <p>Please log in.</p>
{% endif %}
```

- **Including Templates**: You can include other templates within your current template using the {% include %} tag.

html
Copy code
```
{% include 'sidebar.html' %}
```

This allows you to break your templates into smaller, reusable components.

# Using Template Filters

Template filters are another powerful feature in Django's templating system, allowing you to modify variables before displaying them. Filters are applied using the pipe (|) syntax.

## Common Filters

Some common template filters include:

- **date**: Formats date objects.

html
Copy code
```
<p>Published on: {{ post.created_at|date:"F j, Y" }}</p>
```

- **length**: Returns the length of a list or string.

html
Copy code
```
<p>Total posts: {{ posts|length }}</p>
```

- **lower**: Converts a string to lowercase.

html
Copy code
```
<p>{{ post.title|lower }}</p>
```

## Creating Custom Template Filters

You can also create custom template filters to suit your needs. To do this, create a new file named templatetags within your app directory, and define your filters there.

1. **Create a new directory named templatetags in your app:**

plaintext
Copy code
```
myapp/
    templatetags/
        __init__.py
        custom_filters.py
```

2. **Define your custom filter in custom_filters.py:**

python
Copy code
```python
from django import template

register = template.Library()

@register.filter
def truncatewords(value, arg):
    return ' '.join(value.split()[:arg])
```

3. **Use your custom filter in a template:**

html
Copy code
```html
<p>{{ post.content|truncatewords:30 }}</p>
```

This custom filter, truncatewords, allows you to limit the number of words displayed from the content.

# Template Context Processors

Django allows you to define context processors that inject data into all templates. This is useful for making variables, such as the currently logged-in user or site-wide settings, available across all templates.

## Creating a Context Processor

To create a context processor, define a function that returns a dictionary of data and place it in one of your app's files (usually context_processors.py).

python
Copy code
```python
def site_settings(request):
    return {
        'site_name': 'My Blog',
```

```
    'author': 'Your Name',
}
```

Next, add your context processor to the TEMPLATES setting in settings.py:

python
Copy code
```
TEMPLATES = [
    {
        ...
        'OPTIONS': {
            'context_processors': [
                ...
                'myapp.context_processors.site_settings',
            ],
        },
    },
]
```

Now, you can access site_name and author in any template without needing to pass them from a view.

# Conclusion of Chapter 7

Django's templating system and template inheritance provide a flexible and powerful way to create dynamic web pages. By understanding how to use templates, implement inheritance, and leverage template tags and filters, you can efficiently manage the presentation layer of your application. This separation of concerns enables you to create maintainable and scalable web applications, setting a strong foundation for further development in Django.

# Chapter 8: Django Forms and Validation

Forms are an essential component of web applications, allowing users to input and submit data. Django provides a robust forms framework that simplifies form creation, handling, and validation. This chapter explores how to create forms in Django, validate user input, and manage form submissions.

## Creating Forms in Django

Django forms are defined using the forms module, which provides a high-level abstraction for handling form data. You can create forms by defining a class that inherits from django.forms.Form or django.forms.ModelForm.

### Basic Forms

To create a simple form, start by importing forms from Django:

python
Copy code
```
from django import forms
```

```python
class ContactForm(forms.Form):
    name = forms.CharField(max_length=100)
    email = forms.EmailField()
    message = forms.CharField(widget=forms.Textarea)
```

In this example, the ContactForm class defines three fields: name, email, and message. Each field is represented by an instance of a form field class, such as CharField and EmailField. You can also customize the widgets used to render the fields by passing the widget argument.

## Using ModelForms

For forms that correspond to database models, Django provides ModelForm, which automatically generates fields based on your model's fields. Here's how to create a ModelForm for a Post model:

python
Copy code
```python
from django import forms
from .models import Post

class PostForm(forms.ModelForm):
    class Meta:
        model = Post
```

```
fields = ['title', 'content']
```

In this case, the PostForm will generate fields for title and content, and it will handle the associated validation and rendering.

## Rendering Forms in Templates

To render a form in a template, you can use the {{ form }} syntax, which outputs the form fields and associated HTML. Here's an example of how to render the ContactForm:

html
Copy code
```
<form method="post">
    {% csrf_token %}
    {{ form.as_p }}
    <button type="submit">Submit</button>
</form>
```

The {{ form.as_p }} method renders each field as a paragraph, including any validation errors. The {% csrf_token %} tag protects against Cross-Site Request Forgery attacks by including a token in the form.

# Handling Form Submissions

To process form submissions, you typically check if the request method is POST and then validate the form. Here's how to handle the ContactForm in a view:

python
Copy code
```
from django.shortcuts import render
from .forms import ContactForm

def contact_view(request):
    if request.method == 'POST':
        form = ContactForm(request.POST)
        if form.is_valid():
            # Process the data in form.cleaned_data
            # For example, send an email
            return redirect('success')  # Redirect after a successful submission
    else:
        form = ContactForm()

    return render(request, 'contact.html', {'form': form})
```

In this example, if the form is valid, you can access the cleaned data through form.cleaned_data, which is a dictionary containing the validated form fields. After processing the data, you typically redirect to another page to prevent resubmission.

# Form Validation

Django provides built-in validation for common field types, but you can also implement custom validation logic. Validation occurs when you call form.is_valid(), which checks each field against its validation rules.

### Field Validation

Each form field in Django has its own validation rules. For instance, the EmailField will automatically validate that the input is a valid email address. If validation fails, the errors are stored in form.errors.

You can also specify custom validation rules by defining a clean_<fieldname>() method in your form class. For example, you could validate the name field like this:

python
Copy code
```
class ContactForm(forms.Form):
    name = forms.CharField(max_length=100)
```

```python
def clean_name(self):
    name = self.cleaned_data.get('name')
    if not name.isalpha():
        raise forms.ValidationError("Name should contain only letters.")
    return name
```

In this case, the `clean_name` method checks if the name contains only alphabetic characters. If it doesn't, it raises a `ValidationError`, and the error message will be displayed in the form.

## Form-Wide Validation

You can also implement form-wide validation by defining a `clean()` method in your form. This method can validate multiple fields at once:

python
Copy code
```python
class ContactForm(forms.Form):
    email = forms.EmailField()
    message = forms.CharField(widget=forms.Textarea)

    def clean(self):
        cleaned_data = super().clean()
        email = cleaned_data.get('email')
        message = cleaned_data.get('message')
```

```python
if email and "spam" in message:
    raise forms.ValidationError("Messages cannot contain the word 'spam'.")
```

In this example, the clean() method checks if the message contains the word "spam" and raises a validation error if it does.

## Displaying Validation Errors

When rendering forms in templates, you should display validation errors to inform users about incorrect input. You can access errors for each field using {{ form.field_name.errors }}. Here's how to modify the contact form template to display errors:

html
Copy code
```html
<form method="post">
    {% csrf_token %}
    {{ form.name.label }} {{ form.name }} {% for error in form.name.errors %}<span>{{ error }}</span>{% endfor %}
    <br>
```

```
    {{ form.email.label }} {{ form.email }} {% for error
in form.email.errors %}<span>{{ error }}</span>{%
endfor %}
    <br>
    {{ form.message.label }} {{ form.message }} {% for
error in form.message.errors %}<span>{{ error
}}</span>{% endfor %}
    <br>
    <button type="submit">Submit</button>
</form>
```

In this example, the template iterates over each field's errors and displays them next to the respective input field.

# Working with Formsets

Django also supports formsets, which allow you to manage multiple instances of a form on a single page. This is particularly useful for scenarios like managing a list of related items. To create a formset, you can use formsets from django.forms.

### Creating a Formset

First, define a standard form and then create a formset based on that form:

python
Copy code
```
from django.forms import modelformset_factory
from .models import Post

PostFormSet = modelformset_factory(Post, fields=('title', 'content'), extra=3)
```

In this example, PostFormSet will generate a formset with three empty forms for creating new Post instances.

## Rendering and Handling Formsets

You can render a formset in your template similarly to a standard form:

html
Copy code
```
<form method="post">
    {% csrf_token %}
    {{ formset.management_form }}
    {% for form in formset %}
        {{ form.as_p }}
    {% endfor %}
    <button type="submit">Save</button>
</form>
```

In the view, you would handle formset submissions like this:

python
Copy code
```
def post_bulk_create_view(request):
    if request.method == 'POST':
        formset = PostFormSet(request.POST)
        if formset.is_valid():
            formset.save()
            return redirect('success')
    else:
        formset = PostFormSet(queryset=Post.objects.none())

    return render(request, 'post_bulk_create.html', {'formset': formset})
```

This view processes the formset submission, validates the data, and saves it to the database if everything is correct.

## Conclusion of Chapter 8

Django forms provide a powerful mechanism for handling user input and validation in web applications. By utilizing Django's form framework, you can easily create, render, and validate forms, making user interaction seamless and intuitive. Whether you're building simple contact forms or complex multi-part forms, Django's tools simplify the process and enhance the user experience. Understanding how to work with forms and formsets equips you with the skills to create dynamic web applications that meet user needs effectively.

# Chapter 9: Django Models and Database Management

Django's models provide a powerful and flexible way to interact with your database. They serve as the foundation for your application's data structure, allowing you to define the types of data your application will handle, how it is stored, and the relationships between different data types. This chapter delves into how to create models, manage database migrations, and utilize Django's ORM (Object-Relational Mapping) to interact with your database.

## Defining Models

In Django, models are defined as Python classes that subclass django.db.models.Model. Each class represents a table in the database, and the attributes of the class correspond to the fields in that table.

**Creating a Basic Model**

To create a model, you start by importing the necessary modules from Django:

python
Copy code
```
from django.db import models

class Post(models.Model):
    title = models.CharField(max_length=200)
    content = models.TextField()
    created_at = models.DateTimeField(auto_now_add=True)
    updated_at = models.DateTimeField(auto_now=True)

    def __str__(self):
        return self.title
```

In this example, the Post model has four fields: title, content, created_at, and updated_at. The CharField and TextField are used for string data, while DateTimeField is utilized for timestamping the creation and updates of the post. The __str__ method returns a human-readable string representation of the model, which is useful for displaying model instances in the Django admin interface.

## Field Types

Django provides a wide variety of field types to suit different data needs:

- **CharField**: A field for short strings, such as titles or names.
- **TextField**: A field for longer text, like blog posts or comments.
- **IntegerField**: A field for integer values.
- **BooleanField**: A field for true/false values.
- **EmailField**: A field specifically for email addresses.
- **DateField and DateTimeField**: Fields for storing date and date/time information.
- **ForeignKey**: A field that creates a many-to-one relationship between models.

## Relationships Between Models

Django allows you to define relationships between models using ForeignKey, OneToOneField, and ManyToManyField.

- **ForeignKey**: Creates a many-to-one relationship. For example, if you have an Author model, you could link it to Post like this:

python
Copy code

```python
class Author(models.Model):
    name = models.CharField(max_length=100)

class Post(models.Model):
    title = models.CharField(max_length=200)
    author = models.ForeignKey(Author, on_delete=models.CASCADE)
```

In this case, each post can have one author, while each author can have multiple posts.

- **OneToOneField**: Represents a one-to-one relationship between two models. This is useful for extending the functionality of an existing model.
- **ManyToManyField**: Creates a many-to-many relationship. For instance, if you have a Tag model, you could associate tags with posts like this:

python
Copy code
```python
class Tag(models.Model):
    name = models.CharField(max_length=50)

class Post(models.Model):
    title = models.CharField(max_length=200)
    tags = models.ManyToManyField(Tag)
```

Here, each post can have multiple tags, and each tag can be associated with multiple posts.

# Database Migrations

Django uses migrations to propagate changes you make to your models into the database schema. Migrations are a way to apply database changes in a structured manner, allowing you to create, alter, and delete database tables without losing data.

### Creating Migrations

Whenever you create or modify a model, you need to create a migration file. This can be done using the following command:

bash
Copy code
```
python manage.py makemigrations
```

This command scans your models and generates migration files that describe the changes. Each migration file is timestamped and contains a series of operations to apply to the database.

## Applying Migrations

To apply the migrations to the database, use the following command:

bash
Copy code
```
python manage.py migrate
```

This command reads the migration files and applies them to the database, creating or modifying tables as specified.

## Managing Migrations

You can view the current status of your migrations with:

bash
Copy code
```
python manage.py showmigrations
```

If you ever need to roll back migrations, you can do so with the following command:

bash
Copy code
```
python manage.py migrate app_name migration_name
```

This command allows you to revert to a specific migration state.

# Using Django's ORM

Django's Object-Relational Mapping (ORM) provides a powerful interface for interacting with your database using Python code instead of raw SQL queries. The ORM abstracts the complexity of database operations, allowing you to focus on your application's logic.

## Creating and Saving Instances

To create and save a new instance of a model, you can do the following:

python
Copy code
```
post = Post(title="My First Post", content="This is the content of my first post.")
post.save()
```

Alternatively, you can use the create() method, which creates and saves an instance in one step:

python
Copy code
```
post = Post.objects.create(title="My First Post", content="This is the content of my first post.")
```

## Querying the Database

Django's ORM makes it easy to retrieve data from the database. You can use various query methods provided by the QuerySet API:

- **Retrieving All Objects**:

python
Copy code
```
all_posts = Post.objects.all()
```

- **Filtering Objects**:

python
Copy code
```
recent_posts = Post.objects.filter(created_at__gte='2024-01-01')
```

- **Getting a Single Object**:

python

```
Copy code
try:
    post = Post.objects.get(id=1)
except Post.DoesNotExist:
    post = None
```

- **Ordering Objects**:

python
Copy code
```
ordered_posts = Post.objects.order_by('-created_at')  # Descending order
```

- **Chaining Queries**: You can chain filters and other methods to refine your queries:

python
Copy code
```
recent_posts = Post.objects.filter(author=author).order_by('-created_at')
```

## Updating and Deleting Instances

You can easily update or delete model instances using the ORM. To update an instance:

python

Copy code
```
post = Post.objects.get(id=1)
post.title = "Updated Title"
post.save()
```

To delete an instance:

python
Copy code
```
post = Post.objects.get(id=1)
post.delete()
```

Alternatively, you can delete objects directly from the query set:

python
Copy code
```
Post.objects.filter(created_at__lt='2024-01-01').delete()
```

# Customizing Model Behavior

Django allows you to customize the behavior of your models through various methods and properties.

### Model Methods

You can add custom methods to your model classes to encapsulate related logic. For example, you might want to add a method to retrieve a summary of a post:

python
Copy code
```
class Post(models.Model):
    title = models.CharField(max_length=200)
    content = models.TextField()

    def get_summary(self):
        return self.content[:100]  # Return the first 100 characters
```

## Meta Options

You can customize various aspects of your model by defining an inner Meta class. This allows you to specify options such as the default ordering of records, verbose names, and more:

python
Copy code
```
class Post(models.Model):
    title = models.CharField(max_length=200)

    class Meta:
```

```python
    ordering = ['-created_at']
    verbose_name = "Blog Post"
    verbose_name_plural = "Blog Posts"
```

# Database Relationships in the Admin Interface

Django's admin interface is automatically generated based on your models, allowing you to manage your data easily. When you define relationships between models, Django provides intuitive ways to navigate and manage related data in the admin.

## Inline Models

If you want to manage related objects directly from the parent object's admin page, you can use inline models. For example, if you have a Comment model related to the Post model, you can define an inline for the comments:

python
Copy code
```python
from django.contrib import admin
from .models import Post, Comment

class CommentInline(admin.TabularInline):
```

```python
    model = Comment
    extra = 1  # Number of empty forms to display

class PostAdmin(admin.ModelAdmin):
    inlines = [CommentInline]

admin.site.register(Post, PostAdmin)
```

This setup allows you to add or edit comments directly on the post's admin page.

# Conclusion of Chapter 9

Django models and database management provide a robust framework for defining, managing, and interacting with your application's data. By leveraging Django's ORM, you can easily create, read, update, and delete data without needing to write raw SQL. Understanding how to effectively use models, migrations, and relationships equips you with the skills to build data-driven applications efficiently. As you continue to explore Django, this foundational knowledge will serve as a vital component of your development toolkit.

# Chapter 10: Django Admin Interface and Customization

Django's built-in admin interface is one of its standout features, providing a powerful and intuitive way to manage your application's data. This chapter explores how to configure the Django admin interface, customize its appearance and behavior, and enhance it with additional functionality.

## Setting Up the Admin Interface

To access the Django admin interface, you first need to ensure that it is included in your project. Django comes with an admin app that you must add to your INSTALLED_APPS setting if it's not already there:

python
Copy code
```
INSTALLED_APPS = [
    ...
    'django.contrib.admin',
```

...
]

Once the admin app is enabled, you can create a superuser account to log into the admin interface. Use the following command to create a superuser:

bash
Copy code
```
python manage.py createsuperuser
```

Follow the prompts to enter a username, email, and password. After creating the superuser, start your development server:

bash
Copy code
```
python manage.py runserver
```

You can now access the admin interface at http://127.0.0.1:8000/admin/ and log in with your superuser credentials.

# Registering Models in the Admin

To make your models accessible in the admin interface, you need to register them. This is typically done in the admin.py file within your app. Here's how to register the Post model:

```python
Copy code
from django.contrib import admin
from .models import Post

admin.site.register(Post)
```

Once registered, the Post model will appear in the admin interface, allowing you to create, edit, and delete instances of that model.

# Customizing the Admin Interface

Django provides several options for customizing the appearance and functionality of the admin interface. You can enhance user experience by configuring list displays, filters, search fields, and more.

## Customizing Model Admin Classes

To customize the behavior of the admin interface for a specific model, you can define a custom

ModelAdmin class. Here's how to customize the PostAdmin class:

python
Copy code
```
from django.contrib import admin
from .models import Post

class PostAdmin(admin.ModelAdmin):
    list_display = ('title', 'created_at', 'updated_at')
    search_fields = ('title',)
    list_filter = ('created_at',)
    ordering = ('-created_at',)

admin.site.register(Post, PostAdmin)
```

In this example, list_display specifies which fields should be displayed in the list view, search_fields enables a search box for the title field, list_filter adds filters for narrowing down results, and ordering determines the default sorting order.

## Adding Inline Models

If your model has related models, you can include them inline within the parent model's admin page. This is particularly useful for managing related data without navigating to different pages. For example, if you have a Comment model related to Post, you can use an inline model:

python
Copy code

```python
from django.contrib import admin
from .models import Post, Comment

class CommentInline(admin.TabularInline):
    model = Comment
    extra = 1  # Number of empty forms to display

class PostAdmin(admin.ModelAdmin):
    inlines = [CommentInline]

admin.site.register(Post, PostAdmin)
```

With this setup, you can manage comments directly from the post's admin page.

## Customizing Admin Forms

You can customize the forms used in the admin interface to improve the user experience. This can involve changing field layouts, adding custom widgets, or implementing custom validation.

## Customizing Fieldsets

To customize the layout of fields in the admin form, you can use the fieldsets attribute:

python
Copy code
```
class PostAdmin(admin.ModelAdmin):
    fieldsets = (
        (None, {
            'fields': ('title', 'content')
        }),
        ('Dates', {
            'fields': ('created_at', 'updated_at'),
            'classes': ('collapse',)  # Collapsible section
        }),
    )
```

This example groups the fields into sections, making the form easier to navigate.

## Customizing Widgets

You can also customize the widgets used for input fields in the admin forms:

python
Copy code

```python
from django import forms

class PostAdminForm(forms.ModelForm):
    class Meta:
        model = Post
        fields = '__all__'
        widgets = {
            'content': forms.Textarea(attrs={'rows': 5, 'cols': 20}),
        }

class PostAdmin(admin.ModelAdmin):
    form = PostAdminForm
```

This approach allows you to specify custom attributes for input fields, enhancing usability.

# Adding Actions in the Admin Interface

Django allows you to define custom actions that can be applied to multiple selected objects in the admin list view. Actions are useful for performing bulk operations on selected items.

## Defining Custom Actions

You can define a custom action within your ModelAdmin class:

python
Copy code
```python
class PostAdmin(admin.ModelAdmin):
    actions = ['mark_published']

    def mark_published(self, request, queryset):
        queryset.update(status='published')  # Assume there's a 'status' field
        self.message_user(request, "Selected posts have been marked as published.")

    mark_published.short_description = "Mark selected posts as published"
```

In this example, the mark_published action updates the status field for all selected posts. The short_description attribute provides a human-readable name for the action in the admin interface.

## Customizing the Admin Site

You can further customize the overall appearance and behavior of the Django admin site by overriding various settings and attributes.

## Changing the Admin Site Header

To change the site header, you can modify the AdminSite class:

python
Copy code
```
from django.contrib import admin

admin.site.site_header = "My Blog Admin"
admin.site.site_title = "Blog Admin Portal"
admin.site.index_title = "Welcome to the Blog Administration"
```

These attributes change the text displayed in the admin header, title, and index page.

## Styling the Admin Interface

If you want to customize the appearance of the admin interface beyond what Django offers by default, you can include your CSS styles. Create a static directory and include your custom CSS files.

1. **Create a CSS File**: Place your CSS file in a static directory, e.g., static/admin_custom.css.

2. **Load the CSS in the Admin**: Override the change_form.html template to include your CSS file:

python
Copy code
```
from django.contrib import admin

class CustomAdmin(admin.ModelAdmin):
    class Media:
        css = {
            'all': ('admin_custom.css',)
        }
```

This allows you to apply your styles to the admin interface, enhancing its appearance and usability.

# Implementing Custom Permissions

Django's admin interface supports a permissions framework that allows you to control access to specific models and actions. You can customize permissions to ensure that only authorized users can perform certain actions.

## Custom Permissions on Models

You can define custom permissions directly in your model class using the Meta inner class:

python
Copy code
```python
class Post(models.Model):
    title = models.CharField(max_length=200)

    class Meta:
        permissions = [
            ("can_publish", "Can publish posts"),
            ("can_edit", "Can edit posts"),
        ]
```

With these permissions defined, you can assign them to users or groups in the admin interface.

## Restricting Actions Based on Permissions

In your ModelAdmin, you can restrict actions based on the permissions defined:

python
Copy code
```python
class PostAdmin(admin.ModelAdmin):
    actions = ['publish_posts']

    def publish_posts(self, request, queryset):
```

```python
    if not request.user.has_perm('myapp.can_publish'):
        self.message_user(request, "You do not have permission to publish posts.")
        return
    queryset.update(status='published')
    self.message_user(request, "Selected posts have been published.")
```

This ensures that only users with the appropriate permissions can execute the action.

# Extending the Admin with Third-Party Packages

Django's admin interface can be extended with various third-party packages that provide additional functionality or improve the admin experience.

### Django Grappelli

Django Grappelli is a popular third-party package that enhances the Django admin interface with a modern look and additional features. It provides a responsive layout, improved navigation, and customizable themes.

To install Grappelli, add it to your INSTALLED_APPS:

python
Copy code
```
INSTALLED_APPS = [
    'grappelli',
    'django.contrib.admin',
    ...
]
```

Then run `python manage.py collectstatic` to collect the static files.

## Django Suit

Django Suit is another package that offers a sleek, modern admin interface. It provides features like dashboard widgets, improved forms, and better navigation.

To install Django Suit, add it to your INSTALLED_APPS:

python
Copy code
```
INSTALLED_APPS = [
    'django.contrib.admin',
```

```
'suit',
...
]
```

# Conclusion of Chapter 10

Django's admin interface is a powerful tool for managing your application's data. By understanding how to configure, customize, and extend the admin interface, you can create a user-friendly experience for administrators and content managers. The built-in features, along with the ability to define custom actions, permissions, and styling, make the Django admin a vital part of your development toolkit. Whether you are managing a simple blog or a complex application, mastering the Django admin interface will significantly enhance your workflow and data management capabilities.

# Chapter 11: Building RESTful APIs with Django Rest Framework

Django Rest Framework (DRF) is a powerful toolkit for building Web APIs in Django. This chapter explores the core concepts of DRF, including serializers, views, authentication, and permissions, enabling you to create robust and scalable RESTful APIs.

## Understanding RESTful APIs

REST (Representational State Transfer) is an architectural style that defines a set of constraints for creating web services. RESTful APIs allow clients to interact with server-side resources using standard HTTP methods such as GET, POST, PUT, PATCH, and DELETE.

### Key Principles of REST

RESTful APIs adhere to several principles:

- **Statelessness**: Each request from a client contains all the information needed to

understand and process it, without relying on stored context on the server.
- **Resource-Based**: APIs are designed around resources, typically represented as URLs. Each resource is identified by a unique URI.
- **Use of Standard HTTP Methods**: REST APIs utilize standard HTTP methods to perform operations on resources, following predictable conventions.

# Setting Up Django Rest Framework

To begin using DRF, you first need to install it. You can do this using pip:

bash
Copy code
```
pip install djangorestframework
```

Next, add 'rest_framework' to your INSTALLED_APPS in settings.py:

python
Copy code
```
INSTALLED_APPS = [
```

```
...
'rest_framework',
]
```

# Creating Your First API Endpoint

To create an API endpoint, you typically define a model, create a serializer for that model, and then implement views to handle incoming requests.

### Defining a Model

Let's say you want to create an API for a Post model:

python
Copy code
```
from django.db import models

class Post(models.Model):
    title = models.CharField(max_length=200)
    content = models.TextField()
    created_at = models.DateTimeField(auto_now_add=True)

    def __str__(self):
        return self.title
```

## Creating a Serializer

A serializer in DRF is used to convert complex data types, such as querysets and model instances, into JSON format. You define a serializer for your model as follows:

python
Copy code
```
from rest_framework import serializers

class PostSerializer(serializers.ModelSerializer):
    class Meta:
        model = Post
        fields = '__all__'  # Include all fields
```

## Creating API Views

DRF provides several types of views, including function-based views and class-based views. Here's how to create a simple API view using a class-based approach:

python
Copy code
```
from rest_framework import generics
```

```python
from .models import Post
from .serializers import PostSerializer

class PostListCreate(generics.ListCreateAPIView):
    queryset = Post.objects.all()
    serializer_class = PostSerializer
```

In this example, ListCreateAPIView provides both GET and POST functionality for listing posts and creating a new post.

## Configuring URLs

To connect your view to a URL, you need to define a URL pattern. In your app's urls.py, add the following:

python
Copy code
```python
from django.urls import path
from .views import PostListCreate

urlpatterns = [
    path('api/posts/', PostListCreate.as_view(), name='post-list-create'),
]
```

With this configuration, you can now access the API at http://127.0.0.1:8000/api/posts/.

# Handling API Requests and Responses

DRF makes it easy to handle requests and responses in a consistent manner. When a client sends a request to your API, DRF processes the request and uses the appropriate serializer to validate and serialize the data.

### Retrieving Data

When a GET request is made to the /api/posts/ endpoint, the PostListCreate view retrieves all Post instances and serializes them into JSON format, which is returned to the client.

### Creating Data

When a POST request is made to the same endpoint with the new post data in JSON format, DRF automatically validates the incoming data against the serializer. If the data is valid, a new Post instance is created, and a response is returned with the newly created resource.

# Implementing Update and Delete Functionality

To extend your API to handle updating and deleting posts, you can create a view for individual resources.

## Creating a Detail View

You can create a view for retrieving, updating, or deleting a single post:

python
Copy code
```
from rest_framework import generics
from .models import Post
from .serializers import PostSerializer

class PostDetail(generics.RetrieveUpdateDestroyAPIView):
    queryset = Post.objects.all()
    serializer_class = PostSerializer
```

## Configuring URLs for Detail View

In your urls.py, add a new URL pattern for the detail view:

```python
Copy code
urlpatterns = [
    path('api/posts/', PostListCreate.as_view(), name='post-list-create'),
    path('api/posts/<int:pk>/', PostDetail.as_view(), name='post-detail'),
]
```

Now, you can make GET, PUT, PATCH, and DELETE requests to /api/posts/<post_id>/ to retrieve, update, or delete a specific post.

# Adding Authentication and Permissions

Security is an essential aspect of any API. DRF provides built-in support for various authentication methods and permissions to control access to your API.

## Authentication Classes

DRF supports several authentication methods, including:

- **Session Authentication**: Uses Django's session framework.
- **Basic Authentication**: Uses HTTP Basic Authentication.
- **Token Authentication**: Uses a token-based system for stateless authentication.

To enable token authentication, install the djangorestframework.authtoken package and add it to your INSTALLED_APPS:

bash
Copy code
```
pip install djangorestframework.authtoken
```

## Configuring Authentication

In your settings.py, configure the default authentication classes:

python
Copy code
```
REST_FRAMEWORK = {
    'DEFAULT_AUTHENTICATION_CLASSES': [

'rest_framework.authentication.TokenAuthentication',

'rest_framework.authentication.SessionAuthentication',
```

                ],
            }

## Adding Permissions

DRF also allows you to define permissions for your API views. You can specify whether a user must be authenticated or if they require specific permissions to access certain views.

Here's how to add permissions to your views:

python
Copy code
```
from rest_framework.permissions import IsAuthenticated

class PostListCreate(generics.ListCreateAPIView):
    queryset = Post.objects.all()
    serializer_class = PostSerializer
    permission_classes = [IsAuthenticated]
```

In this example, only authenticated users can create or list posts.

# Handling Pagination

When building APIs that return lists of resources, pagination is crucial for improving performance and usability. DRF provides built-in pagination classes that you can configure in your settings.

## Configuring Pagination

To enable pagination globally, add the following to your settings.py:

```python
REST_FRAMEWORK = {
    'DEFAULT_PAGINATION_CLASS': 'rest_framework.pagination.PageNumberPagination',
    'PAGE_SIZE': 10,  # Number of results per page
}
```

## Implementing Pagination in Views

Once pagination is configured, DRF will automatically paginate your list views. When you make a GET request to /api/posts/, the response will include metadata about the pagination, such as the total number of pages and the current page number.

# Testing Your API

Testing is a vital part of API development. DRF makes it easy to test your API endpoints by providing tools for creating automated tests.

**Writing Tests**

You can create tests for your API using Django's testing framework. Here's an example of a simple test case for the Post API:

python
Copy code
```python
from rest_framework import status
from rest_framework.test import APITestCase
from .models import Post

class PostAPITests(APITestCase):
    def test_create_post(self):
        url = '/api/posts/'
        data = {'title': 'New Post', 'content': 'Content of the new post.'}
        response = self.client.post(url, data, format='json')
        self.assertEqual(response.status_code, status.HTTP_201_CREATED)
        self.assertEqual(Post.objects.count(), 1)
        self.assertEqual(Post.objects.get().title, 'New Post')
```

In this test case, we create a new post and verify that the response status code is 201 Created, the post count increases, and the post title is as expected.

## Conclusion of Chapter 11

Django Rest Framework offers a powerful and flexible way to build RESTful APIs with Django. By leveraging DRF's serializers, views, authentication, and permissions, you can create robust APIs that serve a wide range of client applications. Understanding these core concepts allows you to implement best practices for API development, ensuring your APIs are secure, efficient, and easy to use. As you continue to explore DRF, you will be equipped to build APIs that can handle complex data interactions and provide seamless experiences for users.

# Chapter 12: Flask Fundamentals for Web Development

Flask is a lightweight web framework for Python that is widely used for building web applications and RESTful APIs. Known for its simplicity and flexibility, Flask allows developers to get a project up and running quickly while still offering advanced features for scaling applications. This chapter delves into the core concepts of Flask, covering its installation, basic routing, templating, and how to handle requests and responses.

## Setting Up Flask

Getting started with Flask is straightforward. First, you need to install Flask. You can do this using pip:

bash
Copy code
```
pip install Flask
```

Once installed, you can create a simple Flask application. Here's how to set up a basic project structure:

1. **Create a Directory**: Create a new directory for your project.
2. **Create a Python File**: Inside this directory, create a file named app.py.

Now, you can write your first Flask application in app.py:

python
Copy code
```
from flask import Flask

app = Flask(__name__)

@app.route('/')
def home():
    return "Welcome to Flask!"

if __name__ == '__main__':
    app.run(debug=True)
```

In this example, we import the Flask class, create an instance of it, define a route for the home page, and run the application. The debug=True parameter enables debug mode, which provides detailed error messages and automatically reloads the server when code changes are made.

# Understanding Flask Routing

Routing is a core concept in Flask that allows you to define how URLs map to functions in your application. You can create multiple routes that respond to different HTTP methods.

### Defining Routes

In the example above, we defined a route for the home page using the @app.route decorator. You can also create routes for other HTTP methods like POST, PUT, and DELETE. For example, to handle form submissions, you could do the following:

python
Copy code
```
@app.route('/submit', methods=['POST'])
def submit():
    return "Form submitted!"
```

### Dynamic Routing

Flask also supports dynamic routing, where you can capture variables from the URL. Here's how to create a route that takes a variable:

python
Copy code
```
@app.route('/user/<username>')
def show_user_profile(username):
    return f"User: {username}"
```

In this example, `<username>` captures the part of the URL after `/user/` and passes it to the `show_user_profile` function.

# Handling Requests and Responses

Flask provides various ways to handle HTTP requests and construct responses.

### Accessing Request Data

Flask makes it easy to access data sent in requests. You can use the `request` object to get data from forms, query parameters, and JSON bodies:

python

Copy code
```
from flask import request

@app.route('/data', methods=['POST'])
def get_data():
    json_data = request.json
    return f"Received data: {json_data}"
```

In this example, we retrieve JSON data sent in a POST request and return it as part of the response.

## Sending Responses

You can send responses using the return statement. Flask automatically converts Python data types into JSON responses when using the jsonify function:

python
Copy code
```
from flask import jsonify

@app.route('/api/data')
def api_data():
    data = {'key': 'value'}
    return jsonify(data)
```

# Using Templates with Flask

Flask supports templating through the Jinja2 template engine, allowing you to render HTML dynamically based on data passed to the templates.

## Setting Up a Template Directory

To use templates in Flask, create a directory named templates in your project folder. Inside this directory, create an HTML file called home.html:

html
Copy code
```
<!DOCTYPE html>
<html>
<head>
    <title>Flask App</title>
</head>
<body>
    <h1>Welcome to Flask!</h1>
</body>
</html>
```

## Rendering Templates

You can render this template in your Flask application using the render_template function:

python
Copy code
```
from flask import render_template

@app.route('/')
def home():
    return render_template('home.html')
```

This function searches for the home.html file in the templates directory and renders it as a response.

# Working with Forms in Flask

Handling forms is a common task in web applications. Flask provides tools to easily work with HTML forms.

### Creating a Form

You can create a simple HTML form in your template:

html
Copy code
```
<form action="/submit" method="post">
```

```
    <input      type="text"      name="username"
placeholder="Enter your username">
    <input type="submit" value="Submit">
</form>
```

## Processing Form Data

In your Flask view function, you can access the submitted form data through the request.form dictionary:

python
Copy code
```
@app.route('/submit', methods=['POST'])
def submit():
    username = request.form['username']
    return f"Username: {username}"
```

# Handling Errors and Debugging

Flask provides built-in error handling and debugging tools to help you identify and fix issues in your application.

## Error Handling

You can define custom error handlers for various HTTP errors, such as 404 (Not Found) and 500 (Internal Server Error):

python
Copy code
```
@app.errorhandler(404)
def page_not_found(e):
    return "This page does not exist!", 404
```

### Debugging

Running your Flask application in debug mode is crucial during development. When debug mode is enabled, any changes you make to the code will automatically reload the server, and you will see detailed error messages in the browser.

## Structuring a Flask Application

As your application grows, you'll want to organize your code effectively. Flask applications are typically structured in a modular way.

### Creating a Package Structure

A common practice is to organize your application into a package with the following structure:

```
/my_flask_app
    /app
        __init__.py
        routes.py
        models.py
        templates/
        static/
    run.py
```

In this structure, __init__.py initializes the Flask application, routes.py contains the routing logic, and models.py handles database models.

## Initializing the Application

In your __init__.py, you can initialize the Flask app and import routes:

```python
from flask import Flask

def create_app():
    app = Flask(__name__)

    with app.app_context():
```

```
from . import routes  # Import routes
```

```
return app
```

# Integrating with Databases

Flask can easily integrate with various databases. While Flask does not include a built-in ORM, you can use SQLAlchemy, a popular ORM for Python, to manage database interactions.

### Installing Flask-SQLAlchemy

To use SQLAlchemy with Flask, install the Flask-SQLAlchemy extension:

bash
Copy code
```
pip install Flask-SQLAlchemy
```

### Setting Up SQLAlchemy

Configure the database connection in your application:

python
Copy code

```python
from flask_sqlalchemy import SQLAlchemy

app.config['SQLALCHEMY_DATABASE_URI'] = 'sqlite:///mydatabase.db'
db = SQLAlchemy(app)
```

## Defining Models

You can define models as classes that inherit from db.Model:

python
Copy code
```python
class User(db.Model):
    id = db.Column(db.Integer, primary_key=True)
    username = db.Column(db.String(80), unique=True, nullable=False)
```

## Creating the Database

To create the database, you can run the following command in the Python shell:

python
Copy code
```python
from app import db
db.create_all()
```

# Implementing Middleware in Flask

Middleware in Flask is a way to process requests globally before they reach your view functions or after the response is generated. You can use middleware for tasks like logging, authentication, and modifying requests or responses.

## Creating Middleware

You can create middleware by defining a function that takes the Flask application as an argument. Here's an example of a simple logging middleware:

python
Copy code
```
@app.before_request
def log_request_info():
    print(f"Request URL: {request.url}")
    print(f"Request Method: {request.method}")
```

In this example, the log_request_info function is executed before each request, logging the request URL and method to the console.

# Conclusion of Chapter 12

Flask provides a flexible framework for building web applications and APIs with Python. Its straightforward approach, combined with the ability to integrate with various tools and libraries, makes it a popular choice among developers. By mastering the fundamentals of Flask, including routing, templating, form handling, and database integration, you can create powerful web applications that meet the needs of your users. As you continue to work with Flask, you'll discover its capabilities for building complex applications and its suitability for rapid development.

# Chapter 13: FastAPI for Modern Web Development

FastAPI is a modern web framework for building APIs with Python 3.6+ based on standard Python type hints. It is designed to be fast, easy to use, and to enable developers to build APIs quickly with minimal effort. This chapter explores the fundamentals of FastAPI, including its installation, routing, request handling, response models, and how to leverage its powerful features for building robust web applications.

## Getting Started with FastAPI

To begin using FastAPI, you need to install it alongside an ASGI server like Uvicorn. This allows you to run your FastAPI application. You can install both using pip:

bash
Copy code
```
pip install fastapi uvicorn
```

Once you have FastAPI and Uvicorn installed, you can create a simple FastAPI application. Create a file named main.py and add the following code:

python
Copy code
```
from fastapi import FastAPI

app = FastAPI()

@app.get("/")
async def read_root():
    return {"message": "Welcome to FastAPI!"}

if __name__ == "__main__":
    import uvicorn
    uvicorn.run(app, host="127.0.0.1", port=8000)
```

In this example, we import FastAPI, create an instance of it, define a route for the root endpoint, and run the application using Uvicorn.

## Understanding FastAPI Routing

Routing in FastAPI is simple and intuitive. You can define routes using decorators for various HTTP methods like GET, POST, PUT, and DELETE.

## Defining Routes

Just like in Flask, you can create routes for different HTTP methods. Here's how to define a POST route:

python
Copy code
```
@app.post("/items/")
async def create_item(item: dict):
    return {"item": item}
```

In this example, the create_item function accepts a dictionary as input and returns it in the response.

## Path Parameters and Query Parameters

FastAPI makes it easy to work with path and query parameters. You can define dynamic segments in your routes:

python
Copy code
```
@app.get("/items/{item_id}")
async def read_item(item_id: int, q: str = None):
    return {"item_id": item_id, "query": q}
```

In this route, item_id is a path parameter, while q is an optional query parameter.

# Handling Requests and Responses

FastAPI provides a clear and powerful way to handle requests and responses, including validation and serialization.

### Request Body Validation

FastAPI allows you to validate incoming request data using Pydantic models. Here's an example of defining a Pydantic model:

python
Copy code
```
from pydantic import BaseModel

class Item(BaseModel):
    name: str
    price: float
    is_offer: bool = None
```

You can then use this model in your endpoint:

```python
@app.post("/items/")
async def create_item(item: Item):
    return {"item_name": item.name, "item_price": item.price, "is_offer": item.is_offer}
```

In this example, FastAPI automatically validates the incoming request body against the Item model.

## Response Models

FastAPI also allows you to define response models, ensuring that the data returned from your endpoints conforms to a specified structure. You can specify a response model like this:

```python
@app.get("/items/{item_id}", response_model=Item)
async def read_item(item_id: int):
    return {"name": "Sample Item", "price": 10.99, "is_offer": False}
```

Here, the response model ensures that the returned data matches the Item model.

# Using Dependency Injection

FastAPI's dependency injection system is one of its standout features. It allows you to define reusable components for your application.

## Defining Dependencies

You can create a dependency by defining a function that performs some common logic. For example, you might want to handle user authentication:

python
Copy code
```
from fastapi import Depends, HTTPException

def get_current_user(token: str):
    if token != "valid_token":
        raise HTTPException(status_code=400, detail="Invalid token")
    return {"username": "user1"}

@app.get("/users/me")
async def read_current_user(current_user: dict = Depends(get_current_user)):
    return current_user
```

In this example, the get_current_user function checks if the provided token is valid and raises an HTTP exception if it isn't.

# Handling Errors in FastAPI

Error handling is crucial in any web application. FastAPI provides built-in mechanisms to handle exceptions and return appropriate error responses.

**Custom Exception Handling**

You can create custom exception handlers to manage specific error cases:

python
Copy code
```
from fastapi import Request

@app.exception_handler(ValueError)
async def value_error_exception_handler(request: Request, exc: ValueError):
    return JSONResponse(
        status_code=400,
        content={"message": str(exc)},
    )
```

In this example, if a ValueError is raised, the custom handler returns a 400 status code with a message.

## Using Middleware

FastAPI supports middleware, which allows you to execute code before and after the request processing.

### Creating Middleware

You can create custom middleware by defining a function that takes the ASGI application as an argument. Here's an example of logging middleware:

python
Copy code
```
from starlette.middleware.base import BaseHTTPMiddleware

class CustomMiddleware(BaseHTTPMiddleware):
    async def dispatch(self, request, call_next):
        print(f"Request: {request.method} {request.url}")
        response = await call_next(request)
        return response

app.add_middleware(CustomMiddleware)
```

In this middleware, each incoming request is logged before passing it to the next handler.

# Implementing Background Tasks

FastAPI makes it easy to run background tasks, allowing you to offload long-running processes from your request-response cycle.

### Defining Background Tasks

You can use the BackgroundTasks class to run tasks in the background:

python
Copy code
```
from fastapi import BackgroundTasks

def write_log(message: str):
    with open("log.txt", mode="a") as log:
        log.write(message)

@app.post("/send-notification/")
async def send_notification(email: str, background_tasks: BackgroundTasks):
    background_tasks.add_task(write_log, email)
```

    return {"message": "Notification sent in the background"}

In this example, the write_log function runs in the background while the response is returned immediately.

# Integrating with Databases

FastAPI can be easily integrated with databases, using ORMs like SQLAlchemy or Tortoise-ORM.

### Setting Up SQLAlchemy

To use SQLAlchemy with FastAPI, install it along with the database driver:

bash
Copy code
```
pip install sqlalchemy databases asyncpg  # For PostgreSQL
```

### Configuring SQLAlchemy

You can configure SQLAlchemy in your FastAPI application like this:

**python**
Copy code
```python
from sqlalchemy import create_engine
from sqlalchemy.ext.declarative import declarative_base
from sqlalchemy.orm import sessionmaker

SQLALCHEMY_DATABASE_URL = "postgresql://user:password@localhost/dbname"
engine = create_engine(SQLALCHEMY_DATABASE_URL)
SessionLocal = sessionmaker(autocommit=False, autoflush=False, bind=engine)
Base = declarative_base()
```

## Defining Models

You can define your database models using SQLAlchemy:

**python**
Copy code
```python
from sqlalchemy import Column, Integer, String

class User(Base):
    __tablename__ = "users"

    id = Column(Integer, primary_key=True, index=True)
```

    username = Column(String, unique=True, index=True)

## Creating the Database

To create the database tables, you can use:

python
Copy code
```
Base.metadata.create_all(bind=engine)
```

# Testing Your FastAPI Application

Testing is an essential part of the development process. FastAPI provides a built-in test client to simplify testing your endpoints.

## Writing Tests

You can use the TestClient from FastAPI to write tests for your application. Here's an example:

python
Copy code
```
from fastapi.testclient import TestClient
from main import app
```

```python
client = TestClient(app)

def test_read_root():
    response = client.get("/")
    assert response.status_code == 200
    assert response.json() == {"message": "Welcome to FastAPI!"}
```

In this example, we test the root endpoint to ensure it returns the correct status code and response.

# Deploying FastAPI Applications

Once you've built your FastAPI application, you'll want to deploy it. FastAPI applications can be deployed using various platforms and methods.

### Using Uvicorn for Deployment

To deploy your application with Uvicorn, you can run:

bash
Copy code
```
uvicorn main:app --host 0.0.0.0 --port 8000
```

You may also want to use process managers like Gunicorn for production deployments:

bash
Copy code
```
gunicorn -w 4 -k uvicorn.workers.UvicornWorker main:app
```

## Conclusion of Chapter 13

FastAPI offers a modern approach to web development with its powerful features, including automatic validation, asynchronous support, and type hints. By understanding the fundamentals of FastAPI, such as routing, request handling, dependency injection, and database integration, you can build efficient and robust web applications and APIs. Its performance and ease of use make it an excellent choice for both beginners and experienced developers looking to create high-quality web services. As you explore further, you will discover even more capabilities that FastAPI brings to the table for modern web development.

# Chapter 14: Integrating Django and FastAPI for Scalable Applications

Django and FastAPI serve different purposes but can be complementary when building scalable applications. Django excels at providing a comprehensive framework for web development with its ORM, templating engine, and authentication system. FastAPI, on the other hand, is ideal for building high-performance APIs with asynchronous capabilities. This chapter explores how to integrate Django and FastAPI in a single project, discussing the architecture, setting up the environment, routing, and managing shared resources.

## Understanding the Integration Architecture

The first step in integrating Django and FastAPI is to understand the architecture of the application. In this setup, Django typically serves as the primary web framework, handling the front-end and administrative interfaces, while FastAPI manages the API endpoints.

## Microservices vs. Monolithic Architecture

Before diving into integration, it's essential to consider whether you are working within a microservices architecture or a monolithic one. In a microservices approach, Django and FastAPI could be deployed as separate services that communicate via HTTP or a message broker. In a monolithic architecture, you can run both within the same project, sharing the same database and resources.

## Communication Between Services

If using a microservices architecture, you can implement communication between Django and FastAPI using RESTful APIs. Django can send HTTP requests to FastAPI endpoints and vice versa. In a monolithic setup, FastAPI can be added as a module within the Django project, allowing for seamless interaction between Django views and FastAPI routes.

# Setting Up the Environment

Setting up your environment is crucial for a successful integration. You will need to install both

Django and FastAPI, along with an ASGI server like Uvicorn to run the FastAPI application.

## Installing Required Packages

Start by creating a virtual environment and installing Django and FastAPI:

bash
Copy code
```
python -m venv env
source env/bin/activate   # On Windows use `env\Scripts\activate`
pip install django fastapi uvicorn
```

## Creating a Django Project

You can create a new Django project using the following command:

bash
Copy code
```
django-admin startproject myproject
```

Next, navigate into your project directory:

bash
Copy code

cd myproject

## Creating a FastAPI App within Django

Inside your Django project directory, create a new folder for the FastAPI application. For example, you can create a folder named api:

bash
Copy code
```
mkdir api
```

Then create a file called main.py inside the api folder:

python
Copy code
```
# api/main.py
from fastapi import FastAPI

app = FastAPI()

@app.get("/api/data")
async def read_data():
    return {"message": "Hello from FastAPI!"}
```

# Routing in Django and FastAPI

In a project that integrates both Django and FastAPI, you'll need to manage routing effectively. Django handles traditional web routes, while FastAPI will manage API routes.

## Setting Up Django URLs

You can set up Django's routing in urls.py:

python
Copy code
```
# myproject/urls.py
from django.contrib import admin
from django.urls import path, include

urlpatterns = [
    path('admin/', admin.site.urls),
    path('api/', include('api.urls')),  # Include FastAPI routes
]
```

## Creating FastAPI Routes

In your api folder, create a new file named urls.py. This file will be responsible for routing requests to the FastAPI application:

```python
# api/urls.py
from django.urls import path
from fastapi import FastAPI
from fastapi.middleware.wsgi import WSGIMiddleware
from .main import app as fastapi_app

app = FastAPI()
app.mount("/api", WSGIMiddleware(fastapi_app))

urlpatterns = [
    path('', fastapi_app),  # Route for FastAPI
]
```

In this setup, FastAPI is mounted as middleware in Django, allowing it to handle requests at the /api endpoint.

## Managing Shared Resources

One of the advantages of integrating Django and FastAPI is the ability to share resources like the database, authentication, and settings.

### Database Integration

Both Django and FastAPI can use the same database connection. If you're using Django's ORM, you can create models that can be accessed in FastAPI through SQLAlchemy or similar ORMs.

python
Copy code
```
# api/models.py
from django.db import models

class Item(models.Model):
    name = models.CharField(max_length=100)
    price = models.FloatField()
```

You can also access these models in FastAPI:

python
Copy code
```
from .models import Item

@app.get("/items/")
async def read_items():
    items = Item.objects.all()
    return [{"name": item.name, "price": item.price} for item in items]
```

## Shared Settings and Configuration

You can manage shared settings such as database configurations in a single settings file that both frameworks can access. For instance, if you are using Django's settings, you can import them into FastAPI as needed.

python
Copy code
```
import os
from django.conf import settings

DATABASE_URL = settings.DATABASES['default']['NAME']
```

# Authentication and Security

When integrating Django and FastAPI, managing authentication and security becomes essential. Django's built-in authentication system can be used alongside FastAPI's security features.

### Using Django's Authentication System

You can authenticate users in Django and use that information in FastAPI. For example, you can create a Django view that authenticates a user and then allows FastAPI to access the user information.

```python
# Copy code
from django.contrib.auth.models import User

@app.get("/api/user")
async def get_user(user_id: int):
    user = User.objects.get(id=user_id)
    return {"username": user.username}
```

## FastAPI Security Features

FastAPI offers security utilities such as OAuth2, JWT tokens, and basic authentication. You can implement these alongside Django's security features.

```python
# Copy code
from fastapi.security import OAuth2PasswordBearer

oauth2_scheme = OAuth2PasswordBearer(tokenUrl="token")

@app.post("/token")
async def login(form_data: OAuth2PasswordRequestForm = Depends()):
    user = authenticate_user(form_data.username, form_data.password)
```

    return {"access_token": create_access_token(user), "token_type": "bearer"}

# Testing the Integrated Application

Testing is crucial in any software development process. When integrating Django and FastAPI, you should ensure both frameworks function correctly together.

### Testing Django Routes

You can use Django's built-in test framework to test your Django views and routes. For example:

python
Copy code
```
from django.test import TestCase

class MyDjangoTests(TestCase):
    def test_admin_access(self):
        response = self.client.get('/admin/')
        self.assertEqual(response.status_code, 200)
```

### Testing FastAPI Routes

For FastAPI, you can use the TestClient for testing your API endpoints:

```python
from fastapi.testclient import TestClient
from api.main import app

client = TestClient(app)

def test_read_data():
    response = client.get("/api/data")
    assert response.status_code == 200
    assert response.json() == {"message": "Hello from FastAPI!"}
```

# Deployment Considerations

When deploying an integrated Django and FastAPI application, there are several factors to consider. You need to ensure that your server can handle both ASGI and WSGI applications.

## Using ASGI for Deployment

You can deploy both frameworks using an ASGI server like Uvicorn or Daphne. Here's how to run the application using Uvicorn:

bash
Copy code
```
uvicorn myproject.asgi:application --host 0.0.0.0 --port 8000
```

### Using Reverse Proxies

If you decide to deploy Django and FastAPI as separate services, consider using a reverse proxy like Nginx to route requests appropriately. This allows you to manage traffic efficiently between the two applications.

## Conclusion of Chapter 14

Integrating Django and FastAPI opens up new possibilities for building scalable and robust applications. By leveraging Django's features for web development alongside FastAPI's performance for APIs, you can create a powerful and flexible application architecture. Understanding the routing, shared resources, authentication, and deployment strategies will empower you to build high-quality web applications that cater to diverse user needs. The combination of these two frameworks allows developers to harness the best of both worlds, making it an attractive option for modern web development.

# Chapter 15: Building a Full-Stack Application with Django and FastAPI

In this chapter, we will explore how to build a full-stack web application using Django for the backend and FastAPI for the API layer. By combining these two powerful frameworks, we can leverage Django's robust features for managing web pages, user authentication, and database interactions, while using FastAPI's efficiency for handling API requests. We will cover the architecture, setting up the project, creating the frontend and backend, and integrating them effectively.

## Defining the Application Architecture

To build a full-stack application, it's essential to define a clear architecture. The application will consist of three primary layers: the frontend, the backend, and the API.

### Frontend Layer

The frontend will be built using a modern JavaScript framework, such as React or Vue.js, which communicates with the backend through API calls. This separation of concerns allows for a more dynamic and responsive user interface.

**Backend Layer**

The backend will be powered by Django, which will handle user management, data storage, and server-side logic. Django's ORM will allow us to interact with the database efficiently, while its built-in features provide a secure and scalable environment.

**API Layer**

FastAPI will serve as the API layer, providing endpoints for the frontend to interact with the backend. FastAPI's asynchronous capabilities and automatic data validation will enhance the performance and reliability of API interactions.

# Setting Up the Development Environment

To begin building your full-stack application, you need to set up the development environment. This involves creating a virtual environment and installing the necessary packages for both Django and FastAPI.

## Creating the Project Structure

Create a new directory for your project:

bash
Copy code
```
mkdir fullstack_app
cd fullstack_app
```

Then, set up a virtual environment:

bash
Copy code
```
python -m venv env
source env/bin/activate    # On Windows use `env\Scripts\activate`
```

## Installing Django and FastAPI

Install Django and FastAPI along with Uvicorn:

bash
Copy code
```
pip install django fastapi uvicorn
```

## Creating a Django Project

Create a new Django project:

bash
Copy code
```
django-admin startproject backend
cd backend
```

Next, create a Django app for managing your application's core features:

bash
Copy code
```
python manage.py startapp core
```

## Setting Up FastAPI

Inside the `backend` directory, create a folder for FastAPI called `api`:

bash
Copy code
```
mkdir api
```

Inside the api folder, create a file named main.py for your FastAPI application.

# Developing the Backend with Django

In this section, we will develop the backend functionality using Django.

### Defining Models

Start by defining your models in core/models.py. For this example, let's create a simple Item model:

python
Copy code
```
# core/models.py
from django.db import models

class Item(models.Model):
    name = models.CharField(max_length=100)
    description = models.TextField()
    price = models.DecimalField(max_digits=10, decimal_places=2)

    def __str__(self):
        return self.name
```

## Creating Database Migrations

After defining your model, create the database migrations:

bash
Copy code
```
python manage.py makemigrations
python manage.py migrate
```

## Setting Up the Admin Interface

To manage the Item model easily, register it in the Django admin:

python
Copy code
```
# core/admin.py
from django.contrib import admin
from .models import Item

admin.site.register(Item)
```

## Configuring URLs

In backend/urls.py, add a route for the Django admin interface:

python
Copy code
```
from django.contrib import admin
from django.urls import path

urlpatterns = [
    path('admin/', admin.site.urls),
]
```

# Developing the API with FastAPI

Now that we have our Django backend set up, let's develop the API using FastAPI.

## Setting Up FastAPI Routes

In api/main.py, set up FastAPI to handle API requests for the Item model:

python
Copy code
```
from fastapi import FastAPI
from pydantic import BaseModel
from django.core.wsgi import get_wsgi_application
import os
```

```python
os.environ.setdefault('DJANGO_SETTINGS_MODULE', 'backend.settings')
application = get_wsgi_application()

app = FastAPI()

class ItemModel(BaseModel):
    name: str
    description: str
    price: float

@app.get("/api/items/")
async def get_items():
    from core.models import Item
    items = Item.objects.all()
    return [{"id": item.id, "name": item.name, "description": item.description, "price": str(item.price)} for item in items]

@app.post("/api/items/")
async def create_item(item: ItemModel):
    from core.models import Item
    new_item = Item(name=item.name, description=item.description, price=item.price)
    new_item.save()
    return {"id": new_item.id, "name": new_item.name}
```

In this example, the get_items endpoint retrieves all items from the database, while the create_item endpoint allows adding new items.

## Integrating Django and FastAPI

To integrate FastAPI with Django, ensure that the FastAPI application is properly mounted. Update your Django urls.py to include the FastAPI app:

python
Copy code
```
from django.contrib import admin
from django.urls import path
from fastapi import FastAPI
from fastapi.middleware.wsgi import WSGIMiddleware
from api.main import app as fastapi_app

urlpatterns = [
    path('admin/', admin.site.urls),
    path('api/', WSGIMiddleware(fastapi_app)),
]
```

This setup allows the FastAPI app to handle requests made to the /api/ endpoint.

# Developing the Frontend with React

Now that the backend and API are set up, let's create the frontend using React.

## Creating a React App

In the project root directory, create a new React application:

bash
Copy code
```
npx create-react-app frontend
cd frontend
```

## Installing Axios for API Calls

Install Axios to facilitate API calls:

bash
Copy code
```
npm install axios
```

## Creating Components

In the src folder, create a new component for displaying items. Create a file called ItemList.js:

javascript
Copy code
```javascript
import React, { useEffect, useState } from 'react';
import axios from 'axios';

function ItemList() {
  const [items, setItems] = useState([]);

  useEffect(() => {
    async function fetchItems() {
      const response = await axios.get('/api/items/');
      setItems(response.data);
    }
    fetchItems();
  }, []);

  return (
    <div>
      <h1>Item List</h1>
      <ul>
        {items.map(item => (
          <li key={item.id}>
            {item.name} - ${item.price}
          </li>
        ))}
```

```
      </ul>
    </div>
  );
}

export default ItemList;
```

## Rendering the Component

In src/App.js, render the ItemList component:

```javascript
import React from 'react';
import ItemList from './ItemList';

function App() {
  return (
    <div className="App">
      <ItemList />
    </div>
  );
}

export default App;
```

## Proxying API Requests

To facilitate API calls from the React app, add a proxy to the package.json file:

json
Copy code
```
"proxy": "http://localhost:8000",
```

This setup allows the React app to communicate with the Django and FastAPI backend without CORS issues.

# Testing the Full-Stack Application

With both the backend and frontend developed, it's time to test the entire application.

### Running the Django and FastAPI Server

Start the Django server:

bash
Copy code
```
python manage.py runserver
```

Then, run the FastAPI server using Uvicorn:

bash

Copy code
```
uvicorn api.main:app --host 0.0.0.0 --port 8001
```

### Running the React Development Server

In a separate terminal, navigate to the frontend directory and start the React development server:

bash
Copy code
```
npm start
```

# Interacting with the Application

Now that everything is running, you can interact with the application by visiting http://localhost:3000. You should see the list of items fetched from the Django backend via the FastAPI API.

# Deploying the Full-Stack Application

Once you've tested your application locally, it's time to deploy it. You can deploy the Django and FastAPI backend to a cloud provider like Heroku,

AWS, or DigitalOcean. The React frontend can be hosted on platforms like Netlify or Vercel.

### Deployment Steps

1. **Prepare the Backend**: Make sure your Django and FastAPI code is production-ready. Configure settings for production, including allowed hosts and database settings.
2. **Set Up a Database**: If you are using a cloud database, make sure it is set up and connected to your Django application.
3. **Deploy the Backend**: Use a suitable service to deploy your backend application, ensuring it can handle both Django and FastAPI requests.

**Deploy the Frontend**: Build your React application for production:

bash
Copy code
```
npm run build
```

4. Then, deploy the contents of the build folder to your chosen frontend hosting service.

## Conclusion of Chapter 15

Building a full-stack application using Django and FastAPI combines the strengths of both frameworks to create a robust, efficient, and scalable system. By separating concerns into frontend and backend layers, you can take advantage of the best features each framework offers. This architecture allows for

# Chapter 16: API Development Best Practices with FastAPI

Creating robust APIs is essential for modern web applications, and FastAPI provides a powerful platform for developing high-performance APIs. In this chapter, we will delve into best practices for API development using FastAPI, including designing APIs, structuring code, implementing security, validating data, optimizing performance, and documenting your API effectively. By following these best practices, you can build APIs that are secure, efficient, and easy to maintain.

## Designing RESTful APIs

A well-designed API adheres to REST principles, allowing clients to interact with resources effectively. FastAPI supports the creation of RESTful APIs, which use standard HTTP methods to perform CRUD operations.

### Understanding HTTP Methods

The primary HTTP methods used in RESTful APIs include:

- **GET**: Retrieve data from the server.
- **POST**: Create new resources.
- **PUT**: Update existing resources.
- **DELETE**: Remove resources.

When designing your API, choose the appropriate method for each endpoint based on the action it performs.

## Defining Resource URLs

Resource URLs should be intuitive and represent the underlying resources clearly. For example, if you're building an API for a book collection, the following URLs could be defined:

- GET /api/books: **Retrieve a list of books.**
- GET /api/books/{id}: **Retrieve a specific book by its ID.**
- POST /api/books: **Create a new book.**
- PUT /api/books/{id}: **Update an existing book.**
- DELETE /api/books/{id}: **Delete a specific book.**

## Versioning Your API

As your application evolves, you may need to make breaking changes to your API. Implementing versioning helps maintain backward compatibility. You can include the version number in the URL, for example:

- /api/v1/books
- /api/v2/books

This allows clients to continue using the previous version until they are ready to upgrade.

## Structuring Your FastAPI Project

Organizing your FastAPI project helps maintain code readability and manageability. A well-structured project separates concerns and allows for easy navigation.

### Recommended Directory Structure

Consider using the following directory structure for your FastAPI project:

markdown
Copy code
my_project/
    ├── app/

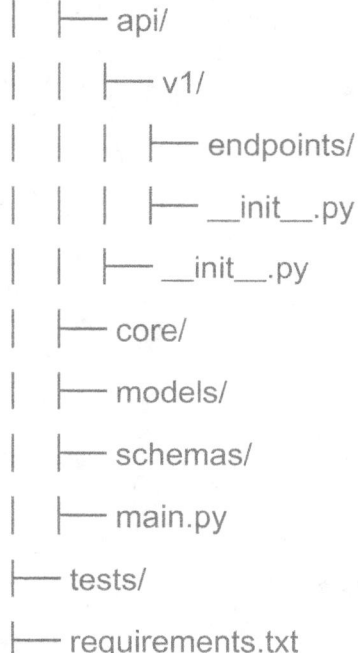
```
|   ├── api/
|   |   ├── v1/
|   |   |   ├── endpoints/
|   |   |   ├── __init__.py
|   |   ├── __init__.py
|   ├── core/
|   ├── models/
|   ├── schemas/
|   ├── main.py
├── tests/
├── requirements.txt
```

## Organizing Endpoints

Within the api/v1/endpoints/ directory, create separate files for each resource. For example, you might have books.py for book-related endpoints. This organization allows you to manage endpoints more easily as your API grows.

## Using Pydantic Models

FastAPI uses Pydantic for data validation and serialization. Define Pydantic models for request and response data to ensure data integrity.

python
Copy code
```
from pydantic import BaseModel

class Book(BaseModel):
    title: str
    author: str
    price: float
```

# Implementing Security

Security is a critical aspect of API development. FastAPI offers various mechanisms to secure your API endpoints.

### Using OAuth2 for Authentication

Implementing OAuth2 allows you to authenticate users securely. FastAPI has built-in support for OAuth2, making it easier to set up.

python
Copy code

```python
from fastapi.security import OAuth2PasswordBearer, OAuth2PasswordRequestForm

oauth2_scheme = OAuth2PasswordBearer(tokenUrl="token")

@app.post("/token")
async def login(form_data: OAuth2PasswordRequestForm = Depends()):
    # Verify user credentials and return a token
    pass
```

## Securing Endpoints

Protect sensitive endpoints by requiring authentication. Use FastAPI's dependency injection to enforce security at the endpoint level.

python
Copy code
```
@app.get("/users/me", dependencies=[Depends(oauth2_scheme)])
async def read_users_me(current_user: User = Depends(get_current_user)):
    return current_user
```

# Validating Data

Data validation is essential for ensuring the integrity and reliability of your API. FastAPI leverages Pydantic for automatic data validation.

## Request Validation

Define request models using Pydantic, which will automatically validate incoming request data.

python
Copy code
```
@app.post("/books/")
async def create_book(book: Book):
    # Book data is automatically validated
    pass
```

## Response Validation

Similarly, you can define response models to ensure that the data returned to clients adheres to the expected structure.

python
Copy code
```
@app.get("/books/{id}", response_model=Book)
async def read_book(id: int):
```

```python
# Retrieve and return book details
pass
```

# Optimizing Performance

FastAPI is designed for high performance, but there are additional strategies you can implement to optimize your API.

## Asynchronous Programming

Take advantage of FastAPI's support for asynchronous programming. By using async and await, you can handle multiple requests concurrently, which improves responsiveness.

python
Copy code
```python
@app.get("/books/")
async def read_books():
    # Simulate a long-running operation
    await asyncio.sleep(1)
    return {"books": [...]}
```

## Caching Responses

Consider caching responses for frequently accessed data to reduce load times. You can implement caching at various levels, such as in-memory caching or using external caching solutions like Redis.

### Using Background Tasks

If you have tasks that can be processed in the background (e.g., sending emails), use FastAPI's background tasks feature to avoid blocking API responses.

python
Copy code
```
from fastapi import BackgroundTasks

@app.post("/send-email/")
async def send_email(email: str, background_tasks: BackgroundTasks):
    background_tasks.add_task(send_email_task, email)
```

## Documenting Your API

Good documentation is essential for API usability. FastAPI automatically generates interactive API documentation using Swagger UI and ReDoc.

## Accessing Automatic Documentation

Once your FastAPI app is running, you can access the interactive API documentation at /docs for Swagger UI and /redoc for ReDoc.

## Adding Descriptions and Metadata

Enhance your API documentation by adding descriptions and metadata to your endpoints and models.

python
Copy code
```
@app.get("/books/", summary="Get a list of books", response_description="A list of books")
async def read_books():
    pass
```

# Testing Your API

Testing is crucial to ensure your API behaves as expected. FastAPI provides testing utilities to help you create and run tests effectively.

## Using TestClient

FastAPI's TestClient allows you to simulate API requests and assert responses.

python
Copy code
```
from fastapi.testclient import TestClient

client = TestClient(app)

def test_read_books():
    response = client.get("/books/")
    assert response.status_code == 200
    assert "books" in response.json()
```

### Writing Comprehensive Tests

Aim to write comprehensive tests covering different scenarios, including success and error cases. Utilize tools like pytest to manage your test suite effectively.

## Conclusion of Chapter 16

By following best practices in API development with FastAPI, you can create robust, secure, and efficient APIs that meet the needs of your applications. From designing RESTful endpoints to implementing security measures, validating data, optimizing performance, and documenting your API effectively, these practices will help you deliver high-quality APIs that enhance the user experience and ensure maintainability. FastAPI's powerful features make it an excellent choice for modern API development, and by leveraging its capabilities, you can build APIs that are both user-friendly and efficient.

# Chapter 17: Deploying FastAPI Applications in Production

Deploying FastAPI applications in a production environment involves a series of steps to ensure that the application is secure, scalable, and performant. This chapter will guide you through best practices for deploying your FastAPI applications, including choosing the right hosting environment, configuring servers, managing dependencies, setting up databases, and implementing monitoring and logging. By the end of this chapter, you will be equipped with the knowledge to deploy your FastAPI applications confidently.

## Choosing the Right Hosting Environment

Selecting the appropriate hosting environment is the first step in deploying your FastAPI application. Depending on your application's requirements, you can choose between various options such as cloud providers, virtual private servers (VPS), and container orchestration platforms.

## Cloud Providers

Cloud platforms like AWS, Google Cloud, and Azure offer flexibility and scalability. They provide managed services for databases, caching, and load balancing, which can simplify deployment.

1. **Amazon Web Services (AWS)**: With services like Elastic Beanstalk and Lambda, AWS supports various deployment strategies, from containerized applications to serverless functions.
2. **Google Cloud Platform (GCP)**: GCP provides services like Google App Engine and Cloud Run, which allow you to deploy applications easily with automatic scaling.
3. **Microsoft Azure**: Azure offers similar services, such as Azure App Service, which enables you to deploy your FastAPI application without managing the underlying infrastructure.

## Virtual Private Servers (VPS)

If you prefer more control over your environment, consider using a VPS. Providers like DigitalOcean,

Linode, and Vultr allow you to configure your server according to your needs. You'll be responsible for managing everything from the operating system to the application stack, which provides flexibility but requires more hands-on management.

### Containerization

Using Docker to containerize your FastAPI application can simplify deployment and scaling. Containers provide a consistent environment that can run on any platform that supports Docker. With container orchestration tools like Kubernetes, you can manage and scale multiple instances of your application effortlessly.

## Setting Up the Server

Once you've chosen a hosting environment, the next step is to set up the server. This process includes configuring the server, installing necessary packages, and setting up a web server to serve your FastAPI application.

### Installing Required Packages

On your server, install the required packages, including Python, pip, and a web server like Nginx or Apache. If you're using a VPS, you might start with a clean Ubuntu or CentOS installation.

bash
Copy code
```
sudo apt update
sudo apt install python3 python3-pip nginx
```

## Configuring a Virtual Environment

It's a good practice to create a virtual environment for your FastAPI application to manage dependencies cleanly:

bash
Copy code
```
pip install virtualenv
virtualenv venv
source venv/bin/activate
```

## Installing FastAPI and Uvicorn

Within your virtual environment, install FastAPI and Uvicorn:

bash
Copy code

pip install fastapi uvicorn

# Deploying the FastAPI Application

Now that your server is set up, it's time to deploy your FastAPI application. You'll need to run the application using Uvicorn and configure it to run in the background.

### Running Uvicorn

You can start your FastAPI application using Uvicorn with the following command:

bash
Copy code
```
uvicorn app.main:app --host 0.0.0.0 --port 8000
```

To ensure that your application runs in the background, you can use a process manager like systemd or supervisor.

### Using Systemd for Process Management

Create a new service file for your FastAPI application:

**bash**
Copy code
```
sudo nano /etc/systemd/system/myfastapi.service
```

**Add the following configuration:**

**ini**
Copy code
```
[Unit]
Description=My FastAPI Application
After=network.target

[Service]
User=yourusername
Group=www-data
WorkingDirectory=/path/to/your/app
Environment="PATH=/path/to/your/venv/bin"
ExecStart=/path/to/your/venv/bin/uvicorn app.main:app --host 0.0.0.0 --port 8000

[Install]
WantedBy=multi-user.target
```

**After saving the file, enable and start the service:**

```bash
sudo systemctl enable myfastapi
sudo systemctl start myfastapi
```

## Configuring a Reverse Proxy with Nginx

To serve your FastAPI application over standard HTTP/HTTPS ports, configure Nginx as a reverse proxy. Create a new configuration file for your application:

```bash
sudo nano /etc/nginx/sites-available/myfastapi
```

Add the following configuration:

```nginx
server {
    listen 80;
    server_name your_domain.com;

    location / {
        proxy_pass http://localhost:8000;
        proxy_http_version 1.1;
```

```
        proxy_set_header Upgrade $http_upgrade;
        proxy_set_header Connection 'upgrade';
        proxy_set_header Host $host;
        proxy_cache_bypass $http_upgrade;
    }
}
```

Enable the configuration and restart Nginx:

bash
Copy code
```
sudo ln -s /etc/nginx/sites-available/myfastapi /etc/nginx/sites-enabled
sudo systemctl restart nginx
```

# Managing Dependencies

Managing dependencies is crucial for the stability and security of your application. Use a requirements.txt file to list your application dependencies.

### Creating requirements.txt

Generate a requirements.txt file by running:

bash

Copy code
```
pip freeze > requirements.txt
```

## Updating Dependencies

Periodically update your dependencies to incorporate security patches and improvements. Use tools like pip-tools or pipenv to help manage dependency versions effectively.

# Setting Up the Database

If your FastAPI application relies on a database, you need to set it up correctly in your production environment.

## Choosing a Database

Select a database that suits your application needs. Popular choices include PostgreSQL, MySQL, and SQLite (for simpler applications).

## Installing Database Drivers

Install the appropriate database drivers in your virtual environment. For example, to use PostgreSQL, install asyncpg or psycopg2:

```bash
Copy code
pip install asyncpg
```

## Database Configuration

Configure your database connection settings in your application. Use environment variables to keep sensitive information secure.

```python
Copy code
import os

DATABASE_URL = os.getenv("DATABASE_URL")
```

# Implementing Monitoring and Logging

Monitoring and logging are critical for identifying issues and maintaining application performance in production.

## Setting Up Logging

FastAPI allows you to integrate Python's built-in logging module. Configure logging to capture important events and errors.

python
Copy code
```
import logging

logging.basicConfig(level=logging.INFO)

@app.get("/items/")
async def read_items():
    logging.info("Fetching items from database")
    # Fetch items logic
```

## Using Monitoring Tools

Consider using monitoring tools like Prometheus, Grafana, or third-party services like New Relic or Datadog to track application performance and resource usage.

## Error Reporting

Integrate error tracking services like Sentry to catch and report exceptions in your FastAPI application. This integration helps identify issues before they escalate.

```bash
pip install sentry-sdk
```

In your application, initialize Sentry:

```python
import sentry_sdk

sentry_sdk.init(dsn="YOUR_SENTRY_DSN")
```

# Ensuring Security Best Practices

Securing your FastAPI application is crucial for protecting sensitive data and preventing attacks.

## Using HTTPS

Serve your application over HTTPS to encrypt data in transit. You can obtain free SSL certificates from Let's Encrypt.

## Environment Variables for Secrets

Store sensitive information, such as API keys and database credentials, in environment variables rather than hardcoding them in your application code.

## Rate Limiting

Implement rate limiting to prevent abuse of your API endpoints. You can use middleware to limit the number of requests a user can make in a given timeframe.

## Regular Security Audits

Conduct regular security audits of your application, dependencies, and server configurations to identify and rectify vulnerabilities.

# Testing Your Deployment

After deploying your application, conduct thorough testing to ensure that everything is functioning correctly in the production environment.

## Functional Testing

Test all API endpoints to confirm that they return the expected results. Use tools like Postman or curl to perform manual testing.

## Load Testing

Perform load testing to evaluate how your application handles high traffic. Tools like Apache JMeter or Locust can help simulate traffic and identify performance bottlenecks.

## Conclusion of Chapter 17

Deploying FastAPI applications in production requires careful planning and execution. By choosing the right hosting environment, configuring servers, managing dependencies, setting up databases, and implementing monitoring and security best practices, you can ensure that your FastAPI applications run efficiently and securely. As you gain experience with deployment, you'll become more adept at handling various scenarios, ultimately leading to a smoother and more reliable application experience for your users.

www.ingramcontent.com/pod-product-compliance
Lightning Source LLC
Chambersburg PA
CBHW052148220526
45471CB00004B/1578